T0256367

Gender and Computers

Understanding the Digital Divide

Gender and Computers

Understanding the Digital Divide

Joel Cooper
Kimberlee D. Weaver
Princeton University

Routledge
Taylor & Francis Group
New York   London

First published by
Lawrence Erlbaum Associates, Inc., Publishers
10 Industrial Avenue
Mahwah, NJ 07430

This edition published 2013 by Routledge

Routledge
Taylor & Francis Group
711 Third Avenue
New York, NY 10017

Routledge
Taylor & Francis Group
27 Church Road
Hove, East Sussex BN3 2FA

Routledge is an imprint of the Taylor & Francis Group, an informa business

Cover design by Kathryn Houghtaling Lacey

Library of Congress Cataloging-in-Publication Data

Cooper, Joel
Gender and computers : understanding the digital divide / Joel Cooper, Kimberlee D. Weaver.
    p. cm.
Includes bibliographical references and index.
ISBN 0-8058-4426-0 (cloth : alk. paper)
ISBN 0-8058-4427-9 (pbk. : alk. paper)
1. Computers and women. 2. Sex differences in education. 3. Computers—Study and teaching. 4. Digital divide. I. Weaver, Kimberlee D. II. Title.
    QA76.9.W65C66 2003
    004'.071—dc21
                                              2003042142
                                                   CIP

Contents

Preface

We do not think it is too dramatic to say that modern western society is at a crossroads in its educational mission. The workplace of the 21st Century is relying on educated citizens who are comfortable with computers and information technology. Children are being introduced to computers at earlier ages with the twin goals of motivating them to learn and to getting them ready to take their place in an increasingly technologically oriented society. An unwritten premise of today's educational mission is that our instruction should motivate and inform all children as equally as possible, without regard to gender, race, or income. These two aspects of the educational mission are currently colliding. There is a well documented digital divide that runs along economic lines. The poor are being left behind. In this book, we document another dangerous divide: Relative to boys, girls are being all too often left behind on the road to technological proficiency.

This book began to take shape at the same time that the technology revolution made its way to the nation's school systems. Advances in computer technology brought with it two major changes in our schools. First, the schools needed to gear themselves for preparing students for the technologically oriented professions of the new millennium. Second, the educational community realized it could bring the sophistication and flexibility of computers to bear on making learning fun and interesting for more and more students. Modeled after the ever-popular video games, classroom computers soon brought all of the bells and whistles of the video arcade to every classroom. Boys came to view the new style of learning with enthusiasm. Learning with the equivalent of joy-sticks and arcade-like metaphors was fun. Girls often came to view it as the source of anxiety.

And so the digital gender divide was born. Boys more rapidly accepted the challenge of becoming computer literate, developing computer skills for the purpose of playing arcade games and perhaps coincidentally for learning the skills that would stand them in good stead for the highly desirable occupations in today's economy. Parents eagerly purchased computers for their sons and encouraged their use. Girls, on the other hand, began to feel that computer skills were not intended for them. Girls rarely found video arcades enjoyable, and they reacted to the transporting of the arcade into the classroom with disdain, distrust, and disaffection. Unlike boys, girls became less interested in academic subjects in school that depended on computer-assisted instruction and unwittingly relinquished their claim to equal partnership with boys for the development of technological skills.

This book is intended as a wake-up call to social scientists, educational practitioners, and parents. It is not too late to remedy the gender divide in technology. But before we can fix it, we must understand it. In this volume, we describe the gender divide in technology, trace its causes in numerous and overlapping social psychological principles, and offer suggestions for change. We explore the causes and consequences of computer anxiety, a strong inhibitor of performance and learning. Girls and women consistently report experiencing more computer anxiety than boys and men, and we examine why. Encouragingly, recent research shows that the way computer classes and environments are structured can alleviate much of this anxiety, and we review techniques that will assist teachers and parents in creating an environment where girls are likely to feel comfortable and succeed. Stereotypes and societal expectancies are another barrier to girls' participation in information technology. If our society believes that computers are the province of men, we, as parents and educators, may unconsciously convey those expectancies to girls that, in turn, lead them to doubt their performance and ability in information technology. Our analysis of the digital divide relies on important concepts that social scientists have studied for some time including self-fulfilling prophecy, stereotype formation, stereotype threat, and attribution theory. We bring these concepts to bear on the problem of the digital divide with two purposes in mind: to identify the causes of the divide and to suggest theoretically derived ways to overcome it.

After analyzing the digital gender divide, we dedicate some time to outlining practical, real-world solutions for remedying the gender gap. These solutions are based on studies of programs that have had success in increasing young women's confidence and lessening their anxiety when working with information technology. In proposing solutions, we also examine a topic that has received much recent media attention, whether math and computer classes should be taught in classes of all girls or all boys. We examine the advantages and drawbacks of single-sex schools and single-sex classes in the context of information technology.

Psychologists and sociologists interested in the social psychological causes of the digital divide will find this book useful. Educators who implement technology policy in the classroom will find important lessons here. And parents will see the importance of making education in computers equally available to their daughters as well as their sons. Those who teach courses in human–computer interaction, human factors, and educational policy will profit from this book. If we successfully communicate the accumulation of research and theory in this area, it will become clear that there exists a substantial problem. It will also become clear that there is no single culprit that created the problem. Similarly, there is no single solution, no magic wand that we can waive to eliminate the gender divide. However, we point to several avenues that we think can lead to genuine change to restore gender equity in computing technology.

Joel Cooper began this project and played a role in much of the research discussed in this book. Kim Weaver joined the project some time later and helped to broaden and expand its scope. Together, we hope we have produced a volume that helps to elucidate the causes of a significant social, educational, and philosophical problem in a way that is both rigorous and accessible.

No book can come together without the help of many people. We gratefully acknowledge: Dink Asano, Michele Bostwick, Barbara Cooper, Grant Cooper, Kim Moss, Andrea LaPaugh, Vera Sohl , Ruth Vellensky, Beverly Weaver and Herbert Weaver. We also thank Lauren, Lida, and the many other students who contributed their time to talk with us about their experiences with computers and technology, and Mark P. Zanna (University of Waterloo), Richard A. Lippa (California State University, Fullerton), Richard S. Sherman (Miami Unviersity of Ohio), and Janet S. Hyde (University of Wisconsin, Madison) for their insightful suggestions.

—Joel Cooper
—Kimberlee Weaver

1

Introducing the Problem

Jared and Martha enter school with a sense of excitement and trepidation. It is September, and the two 5-year-olds are about to enter kindergarten for the first time. Their worlds will be filled with new experiences, from the classroom to the lunchroom, as the long process of formal education begins. Within the next few years, they will understand that the shapes on pages are words and that those words can be read. They will learn the regularities that constitute the study of mathematics, and they will learn the science of the world around them.

Thus it has been for decade following decade. If they are fortunate, Jared and Martha will share with their predecessors an education that features a warm and caring teacher and a supply of appropriate books, paper, and writing implements. However, Jared's and Martha's experiences will diverge from their parents' and grandparents' education in some radically different ways. Unlike their forebears' education, their school will feature the computer, the embodiment of modern technology that many educators believe is in the process of revolutionizing education as we know it. "There won't be any schools in the future," wrote Seymour Papert, the developer of the LOGO computer system, "The computer will blow up the school" ("Trying to Predict the Future," 1984, p. 38).

In the last two decades, computers have proliferated in classrooms the world over. In 1981, for example, fewer than 20% of school classrooms in the United States had computers. By the end of that decade, more than 95% of all classrooms had at least one computer. By the year 2000, virtually all schools owned computers, and 98% were connected to the Internet. The rate at which schools have been purchasing computers has been climbing at greater than 10% per year, with purchases running at approximately $1 billion annually. Unquestionably, computers are becoming a central feature of education from kindergarten to college and beyond. One question that arises from this rapid change is, will Jared and Martha benefit from this new technology? Will the outcome of their education be different in significant ways from that of their parents? Will they learn more or become more motivated to learn on their own because of their exposure to computational technology?

To the casual observer, computers in classrooms may be impressive. But discerning critics, be they parents, teachers or researchers, must look beyond colored screens, sound effects, and moving icons. What can computers teach children? Do computers motivate children to learn more than traditional instructional methods? Has the computer affected children's ability to think in different ways? Does introducing the computer at young ages prepare children better for the workplace of the future?

Computers can add constructively to the educational process both through educational programs designed to motivate children to learn material from traditional disciplines, and also by the inclusion of the computer as a topic of study itself in fields like computer science. The prevalence of computers in modern classrooms and the imposition of computer science requirements in schools mean that Jared and Martha will both spend a considerable amount of time at the machine. However, despite the fact that they will likely have equal access to computers in their classrooms, Jared and Martha will not necessarily be similarly advantaged. If Jared is typical of most boys in Western society, he will have his motivation piqued by the embellishments so cleverly written for the information technology (IT) programs his teachers use to supplement course material. His interest in baseball will motivate him to hit a "home run" by solving an arithmetic problem correctly. His interest in Power Rangers may motivate him to destroy his enemy as he spells a word correctly. Martha, if she is typical of girls in Western society, may not be motivated by the clever metaphors used by the authors of educational IT software to teach course material and the metaphors used by computer programming instructors to teach programming skills. To the contrary, Martha may be motivated to avoid the computer in order to avoid having to play fantasy baseball, having to participate in the violent destruction of invaders from another planet, or having to write a computer program that restricts her to using a rigid and formal programming style.

In this book, we explore the proposition that as things currently stand, computers have the potential for creating inequity both in classroom education in general and in who is encouraged to pursue the study of computer science itself. It is clear that computers do not only educate; they also communicate. And research has shown that boys and girls have not received the communication equally. To the extent that computers are a positive force in education, Jared is more likely to experience the benefits than Martha. Additionally, to the extent that majoring in computer science assures college students a high-paying and interesting career, Jared is more likely to benefit than Martha. Both are correctable problems. But, unless effort is directed toward correcting them soon, parents and educators will face a dilemma in which they find that boys and girls have not received an equally motivating and enriching education. Computers as they are currently structured for use in the classroom may be at fault.

Our main focus in this book is on outlining some of the psychological factors that have contributed to the inequality regarding gender and computers. However, before diving into the research, it will be helpful to take a step back and examine the situation as it stands today.

THE DIGITAL DIVIDE: UNEQUAL ACCESS AND UNEQUAL EFFECTS

Race, Wealth, and the Digital Divide

Education and the workplace have been revolutionized by information technology. The jobs of tomorrow will depend heavily on people's literacy with computers and the Internet. Forecasts are that by the year 2010, 25% of all of the new jobs created in the private and public sectors will be "technologically oriented" (American Association of University Women Educational Foundation Commission on Technology, Gender and Teacher Education, 2000). In both economic upturns and downturns, access to jobs will require training and competency in technology (McClelland, 2001). Yet, access to training in IT is not equitable and some people have greater access than others with the likelihood depending on the income, racial, and gender categories of which people are members. White Americans are more likely to have access to computers and the Internet than African Americans. Males have more access than females, and wealthier Americans have more access regardless of race and gender.

The *digital divide* is a term that has been used to refer to the gap between those who have access to technology and those who do not; between those who have the expertise and training to utilize technology and those who do not. According to Chistopher Latimer in a report to the New York State Forum for Information Resources, social gaps in society cause the digital divide, but the digital divide, in turn, may intensify existing social gaps and create new ones (Latimer, 2001). Because members of minority groups and people from lower socioeconomic groups have less access to technology, they are likely to be even further disadvantaged from attaining some of the higher positions in tomorrow's economy, widening the economic divisions that already exist.

The trend is already occurring. According to a report of the National Science Foundation (Papadakis, 2000), 46.6% of White families in the United States own a home computer, whereas only 23.2% of African American families own one. Although computer purchase and use rose for both Whites and Blacks over the last several years, the *gap* between racial groups has widened. During the 4-year period of 1994–1998, Papadakis reported that computer ownership increased 18% nationally, but the gap between Blacks and Whites widened by an additional 7%. The gap seems to persist at the college level. For instance, the Office of Institutional Research at a community college in northern Virginia polled the commuter-oriented student population and, even among this group, computer ownership was higher among White students than it was among Black students.

Socioeconomic status also plays a large role. Of Americans with incomes of under $15,000, 12.7% have computers in their homes. The percentages climb steadily with income such that families who earn more than $75,000 annually have a 77.7% likelihood of owning a computer. The racial variable is often confounded with income, because Blacks and Hispanics make up a larger proportion of the lower income groups than do Whites. Nonetheless, some racial differences continue to exist, even when income is statistically removed from the phenomenon. For example, the lowest likelihood of computer ownership is for Black households whose income is below $15,000 (7.7%). For all families earning less than $35,000, the percentage of White households owning computers is three times greater than the percentage of Black families and four times greater than the percentage of Hispanic families.

It is not only crucial that everyone has the access and knowledge to use computers and the Internet for the jobs for which they will compete upon finishing school, but it is also critical for school performance itself. Atwell and Battle (1999) examined survey data from a large number of eighth-grade students in the United States. They specifically noted the relationship between a child's having access to a computer at home and their scores on standardized tests. They found that reading and math scores were related to home ownership of computers. Not surprisingly, they also found that White students were more advantaged than Black students; wealthier students were more advantaged than poorer students. More surprisingly, the data showed that, controlling for the number of households who had computers, wealthy students obtained more of an advantage from their computer ownership than did poorer students, and White students obtained more of an advantage than Black students.

The Digital Divide: The Special Case of Gender.   Policymakers have good reason to worry about the digital divide. Wealth and socioeconomic status have frequently made education and employment opportunities more accessible to some than to others. Unequal distribution of wealth, even in the public sector, has created schools that are unequal in facilities, staff, and, in the end, academic performance of its students. The unbalanced relationship between race and socioeconomic status bears prime responsibility for the lower academic performance of traditionally underrepresented minorities. The cycle perpetuates itself as underrepresented minorities are in a disadvantaged position to compete for the higher paying technology jobs of today's and tomorrow's workplace.

The same precipitating factors are more difficult to glean in the case of gender. Nonetheless, compared with men, women are underrepresented in their use and ownership of computers. Women take fewer technology classes in high school and college, are far less likely to graduate college with degrees in IT fields, are less likely to enroll in postgraduate technology fields, and are underrepresented in the higher end of technology jobs. A recent study by the American Association of University Women (AAUW, 2000), for example, highlights how the vast majority of girls and women are being left out of the technology revolution. The AAUW report shows that women and men are using computers as a "tool"—for accessing the Internet, using e-mail, and using word processing programs—at equal rates. However, there is a striking disparity in the number of women and men who are participating in the technological revolution at a more sophisticated level, the level that will allow them to be equal and active participants in the computer revolution that is taking classrooms and workplaces across the world by storm.

Women are conspicuously underrepresented in basic computer science education courses from a young age, and their lack of representation becomes more pronounced as they move through school. In 2001, women made up over 50% of all high school students, but only 17% of the students taking the Advanced Placement Computer Science A test in high school (College Board, 2001). The percentage of women fell to 11% for the more sophisticated Advanced Placement Computer Science AB test.

Only 4% of female college freshmen indicate that they intend to major in computer science (Higher Education Research Institute, 1996). The gender disparity continues through college and on through computer science study at the graduate level. In 1999, despite their equal representation in college overall, women made up only 31% of the students majoring in computer science in the United States (U.S. Department of Education, National Center for Education Statistics, 1999–2000), and received only 16% of the computer science PhDs awarded in 1994 (U.S. Department of

Education, National Center for Education Statistics, 1996). As a direct consequence of the lack of formal computer education and training at the elementary, high school, and collegiate level, women make up only one out of five information technology professionals (American Association of University Women Educational Foundation Commission on Technology, Gender and Teacher Education, 2000). According to many analysts, the number of women entering information technology professions is continuing to decline (Panteli, Stack, & Ramsay, 2001).

The absence of girls and women from computer science classrooms prevents them from participating fully in the "new economy" later on in life and precludes them from earning the high salaries that sophisticated computer skills call forth in today's world. The fact that even more traditional fields of study are using computers to teach children basic materials leads to the possibility that computer assisted education—what the majority of educators believe is the future of education as we know it—has the potential for creating inequity in classroom education

Because the computer revolution is of recent origin, these examples of inequity brought about by computers reflect a relatively new problem. However, it is already the case that educators and researchers face a dilemma of gender inequity in the classroom. The Scholastic Aptitude Test (SAT), one of the most widely used instruments to assess college applicants, already shows reliable and pervasive differences between males and females, particularly in mathematics. This has received both scholarly (e.g., Stricker & Rock, 1995) and political recognition. We think it is clear that the dilemma of gender differences may well be exacerbated by reliance on the computer and the lack of attention paid to the differences in learning styles, motivations, and interests between boys and girls.

Although statistics clearly show pervasive gender inequity in the current computing situation, research has also shown that girls are as competent as boys when computing under certain conditions. As research psychologists, we find this situation an interesting one, because it suggests that there are factors beyond those of innate ability that are playing a large role in the current gender disparities. Martha will happily go to school. If she is prototypical in her attitudes and abilities, she will likely do well in school. If her family has sufficient resources, she will probably have a computer at home and as she grows, she will do her e-mail, correspond with friends, and even play some computer games. However, if she is prototypical, she will not be as excited about computers as Jared will be; she will learn to develop more negative attitudes, will be less likely to take advantage of the computer for her learning and achievement and will be far less likely to avail herself of the opportunities for technology in higher education and the workplace.

Our research and reading of the case research literature on gender and computing has led us to conclude that there are several psychological factors that are at work "behind the scenes" in educational settings that combine to dissuade Martha, and girls in general, from utilizing their full potential when it comes to computers. In this book, we examine these psychological factors in detail in an effort to highlight some of the underlying reasons why the current gender inequalities exist. In so doing, our main focus in this book is on pre-college education, those years when boys and girls are first introduced to computers. However, we focus on these early years with an eye to the fact that they have important consequences for the adult lives of the students. As we examine the psychological factors that underlie the current disparities, we look at whether the promise of computing has gone astray by failing to pay attention to the enormously important issues of equity and fairness. We also propose ways that educators can change the current situation so that both boys and girls are able to take full advantage of all the positive potential computers have for education.

The psychological factors we propose underlie girls' and women's failure to realize their full computing potential can be divided into five areas, and we have dedicated a chapter in this book to a discussion of each. In chapter 2, we begin with a discussion of computer anxiety and the conditions that cause it. Research has shown that on average girls and women experience more anxiety when working with computers than do boys and men. We take a close look at why this is the case, and discuss some psychological research showing that anxiety can be a strong inhibitor of performance and learning. Finally, we wrap up our discussion of computing anxiety with a discussion of how we as educators can introduce computers to children in a way that minimizes anxiety and opens the door to the exciting motivational and intellectual benefits of the computer age for both girls and boys.

In chapter 3, we shift our focus from the psychology behind students' personal relationships with computers and computer software programs to look at how the social context of the computing environment in classrooms influences girls' and boys' experience with computers. Psychological research has taught us that the presence of other people in an environment or a "social context" can have a large impact on people's behavior, attitudes, and thoughts. We argue that the social context that surrounds computing is no exception to this rule. First we look at how social contexts can affect the level of anxiety students feel when working with computer-related tasks. We also discuss research that shows that girls' self-reports of their computer experience and abilities can be influenced by the social context in which they find themselves. Finally, in this chapter we describe research showing that girls perform much better in some social contexts than others, and that educators would do well to take this into account when structuring their classrooms. Chapter 3 also examines the actual social dynamics that come into play in educational computing. Surveys asking teachers to describe how they structure their classrooms indicate that, for a variety of reasons, both financial and pedagogical, teachers tend to have children perform computer-assisted instruction activities in groups. It is not surprising that the composition of the groups matters. The social dynamics that occur within the groups can facilitate or inhibit learning from computer-based instruction. At least three questions arise: What is the gender composition of the groups? What is the mix of abilities in the groups? Is the group learning structured so that the children must cooperate with each other rather than compete with each other? Each of these decisions will have profound impact on the outcome of the learning process. Chapter 3 examines how the dynamic structure of their learning groups determines how much learning and enjoyment boys and girls will experience from their exposure to computers in their classrooms.

In chapter 4, we suggest that one of the major causes of computer anxiety rests in the expectancies that we as a society hold about gender and computer use. We present the results of basic psychological research to show that when people hold expectancies about others, they act in ways that actually bring about the expected behaviors, thoughts, and feelings. Research on the self-fulfilling prophecy has made it clear that people tend to confirm the expectations that others have about them, whether or not those expectancies are true. If we hold the opinion that computers are the province of boys and men, then without necessarily being aware of it, we act in ways to confirm that stereotype. Boys may work harder on the computer; girls may face it with more anxiety and trepidation. Chapter 4 also examines one of the subtle yet invidious consequences of the self-fulfilling prophecy. Believing that computers are for boys and not for girls, society is prepared to accept information technology that appeals to boys ... and not even be aware of it. Moreover, the people who write software for children's education are likely to have the same expectancy about gender and computers. Throughout this volume, we are addressing the consequences of an educational system that relies on male-friendly games and lessons. Why are educational lessons written to be appealing to males? Chapter 4 suggests that we look to the self-fulfilling prophecy for the answer.

Chapter 5 discusses some of the pernicious consequences of societal stereotypes in the context of stereotype threat. Stereotype threat research shows that the mere existence and knowledge of a stereotype causes anxiety in the person who is a member of the stereotyped group. Since girls and young women know that society expects them to perform more poorly at computers, they know that others will interpret their performance through this stereotypic lens. The extra weight or burden of being evaluated through the stereotype can actually lead to poorer performance. In chapter 5, we examine how stereotype threat plays out in the context of gender and computers as well as discuss ways to lessen its influence.

In chapters 6 and 7 we turn our discussion to an examination of potential solutions to the gender gap in science and technology. In chapter 6 we offer concrete ideas to parents and teachers for how to encourage their daughters and female students to identify with computers. Because parents' and teachers' attitudes and opinions directly influence the performance expectations and attitudes their children and students develop for themselves, it is essential that parents and teachers examine their own assumptions about the role that gender takes in technology. In some sense parents are "expectancy socializers," conveying to their children their expectations and hopes and fears. If parents do not believe that their daughters have the ability to succeed at computer tasks, then the girls will take on the same attitudes. Teachers can also play an important role in solving the digital divide by structuring their classrooms in ways that make the girls feel more comfortable using information technology. In chapter 7 we examine in more detail a solution that has recently caught the attention of teachers, parents, and policymakers. Namely, many have recently argued that single-sex classrooms and schools may be one viable solution to the gender gap in science and technology. We examine the advantages and drawbacks of single-sex education, paying specific attention to how separating students by gender might influence the gender divide in technology.

The overall theme of this volume is to suggest that the promise of computers is very real, but it will be an unfulfilled promise if we fail to recognize the serious inequities that exist between boys and girls, men and women, in the ability to profit from the computer. There are also reasons beyond equity and fairness that make such an examination important. Recent news reports have made it clear that the private sector is facing a shortage of technologically skilled workers, and expects the shortage of skilled workers to become greater in the next decade. Certainly encouraging more women to learn the skills necessary to participate in information technology will help to redress this shortage. There are also issues of equality—jobs in information technology are among some of the highest paid professional jobs, and it is unfair for women to be underrepresented in them.

Why is there such disparity in the number of men and women pursuing information technology skills? There are certainly many answers to this question, and in this book we focus on several of the psychological factors that we believe play a role in contributing to and perpetuating the disparity. Throughout the book we also look for insights from research that will help computers fulfill their promise for the vast majority of children.

2

Computer Anxiety: A Matter of Gender

Some years ago, my colleague, Diane Mackie, and I were conducting a study on the effect of violent video games on children's aggressive behavior (Cooper & Mackie, 1986).[1] A middle school in central New Jersey was kind enough to allow us to conduct our study with a class of fifth-grade children. It was our intention to allow the children to play Space Invaders, a game in which the player needs to destroy incoming targets or missiles from enemy space ships, in order to see whether playing the game led children to become more aggressive.

We had anticipated that our presence in the middle school would be an unexpected treat for the children. As stimulating as classroom education may be, it had been our recollection that, when we were in school, some time off to play games was more than welcome. We explained to the children that we were doing a research project, that we were going to have them sit at a computer and play a video game, and that they would then be allowed to go to another room in which there were some attractive toys waiting for them to play with.

It seemed to us that the boys felt they had died and gone to heaven! Here they were, on a regular weekday afternoon, being invited to play video games and then play with toys. They would not have to wait until they arrived home to begin aiming weapons and hitting missiles. Here it

---

[1]Some of the research presented in this book was conducted by Joel Cooper. The use of the personal pronouns *I* and *We* in this context refer to Cooper.

was, in the middle of the school day, in their own school with the blessing of their own teacher.

What we had not expected was the reaction of many of the girls. Ann, an 11-year-old, considered our offer and said politely, "May I go back to my classroom instead? I was reading a story and I would really rather finish it." Then she added, "Besides, my brother plays video games, not me. I'm really not very good at it." When we heard Ann's hesitation, we reassured her that she would do just fine at the game and, besides, it did not matter how she scored or how many missiles she knocked out of the imagined sky. We merely wanted her to play the game as best she could. Ann was extremely hesitant, but eventually came to believe it was easier to get it over with than to continue to plead her case. She played and did remarkably well.

We soon learned that Ann was not to be an isolated case. Hers was only the first of many similar incidents. Some of the girls steadfastly refused to play the game and were allowed to go back to their classroom. Most showed reluctance, but complied with our request. To be sure, some were just as enthusiastic as the boys to play with the video game. But it is clear that we had misgauged the discomfort felt by so many of the girls when they found out they would be spending their time at the video machine rather than doing whatever they had anticipated their classroom activity would have been that spring afternoon.

As we concluded our research that afternoon, we walked along the school corridor on our way to thank the teacher and principal for their co-operation. We gazed into a foreign language classroom and noticed a few boys gathered around a computer terminal, using a game to place the appropriate verb into their French sentences. We passed another classroom in which students were waiting their turn to play a basketball game on their computer as the teaching device for understanding fractions. Again, the line was comprised primarily of boys.

The parallel between the classroom observations and the reactions we had noticed during our aggression study were striking. The fantasies that the majority of girls were reluctant to engage as arcade games were the very same fantasies that were being used by the authors of educational software to "motivate" children to learn French verbs, arithmetic, and presumably much of the rest of the curriculum. And, apparently, the girls were not buying. It was boys who lined up at the computers and boys who thought that it was now fun to engage in these educational activities. The girls were not participating, and we suspect that the fantasy activities on the computer were making their lessons less, rather than more, enjoyable.

If it is true that girls are uncomfortable engaging in video-arcade-type activities, and if it is true that learning on the computer can be a productive and positive experience, then it is predominantly the boys who are receiving the benefit. To take this argument further, it may well be that the positive motivation many girls have for their teachers' lessons is turned into discomfort and reluctance when the lessons are presented by the computer. Rather than increasing learning and motivation, computers may be causing discomfort, negative motivation, and decreased learning for girls.

COMPUTER ANXIETY: A MATTER OF GENDER

Why were the girls in our video game and aggression study reluctant to play the games? What is it about computers that appears to turn girls off? One possibility can be found in the literature on computer anxiety. By the term *computer anxiety* we refer to feelings of discomfort, stress, or anxiety that people experience when responding to computers. Psychological research has shown that there appears to be a relatively high level of computer anxiety in the general population. Despite this high level of anxiety overall, more girls and women suffer from computer anxiety than boys or men.

In this chapter, we review some of the studies that have looked at gender differences in computer anxiety. We consider *why* computer anxiety appears to be a function of gender. Studies on educational software have suggested that the features added to educational computer programs in order to "make learning fun" might be the very thing that leads girls to become anxious when using the computer-based instructional programs. In this chapter, we also argue that computer anxiety may be one reason that girls do not pursue computer programming courses in high school and college. Research examining computer programming styles and gender suggests that the style of programming that is taught and strongly encouraged in today's programming classes may be more in line with the way that boys are used to thinking about and solving problems than the way that girls are. Research has suggested that requiring girls to use a programming style with which they are not comfortable may be another factor that contributes to their increased reports of computer anxiety. After exploring the reasons *why* girls experience more computer anxiety than boys, we will discuss some of the implications that arise from this difference. In particular, we argue that girls' greater anxiety may influence their subsequent attitudes about, identification with, and participation in computer-related activities. With so much of today's educational and business opportunities dependent on computer skills and comfort, this is a problem that dramatically affects modern society.

For the past 20 years, social scientists have been finding evidence for the presence of computer anxiety in the population. Gita Wilder, Diane Mackie, and I surveyed children in the elementary and high school grades (Wilder, Mackie, & Cooper, 1985). We found that a considerable number of children of all ages experienced anxiety about the computer. Gressard and Loyd (1986) found that college students reported being optimistic about computers but nonetheless had a high degree of computer anxiety. Weil, Rosen, and Sears (1987) estimated that approximately one in every three adults suffers from aversive reactions to computers and computer-related technology. Despite the amount of infusion of computers in our lives at the turn of the 21st century, the evidence from recent surveys continues to show that anxiety toward the computer is a major problem that affects people's attitudes (Brosnan, 1998; Chua, Chen, & Wong, 1999).

The tough issue with which society must come to terms is that computer anxiety inequitably affects girls more than boys. Studies from around the world have identified a higher degree of computer anxiety in girls than in boys and significantly more negative attitudes about the computer in girls than in boys. Moreover, these differences occur across a broad age spectrum, beginning in the earliest grades and often increasing in adulthood (Brosnan, 1998; Martin, 1991; Temple & Lips, 1989; Todman & Dick, 1993; Whitley, 1997). As boys grow older, they tend to use the computers they have at home more frequently. As girls grow older, they tend to use their home computers less (Coomber, Colley, Hargreaves, & Dorn, 1997).

Neil Selwyn (1998) interviewed high school students in Great Britain. Fiona, a teenage girl stated, "Computers shouldn't be a male thing but it probably is … when I was playing with dolls my brother was playing on Gameboy and … after you win the game you want to do something more and more and then you've got to get bigger and bigger systems.… They have more interest in the whole thing" (p. 222).

Temple and Lips (1989) assessed computer-related attitudes, comfort, and confidence of more than 300 students at the University of Winnipeg in Canada (see also Brosnan, 1998). Female students rated themselves as less comfortable and less confident about computers than the male students did. Women also reported that they experienced anxiety when contemplating using computers, and that they felt inhibited to pursue careers in technology.

Dambrot and her colleagues (Dambrot, Watkins-Malek, Silling, Marshall, & Garver, 1985) surveyed nearly 1,000 students at the University of Akron. They found that females were more negative in their attitudes and more fearful in their orientation toward computers than were male students. In Spain, Farina, Arce, Sobral, and Carames (1991) assessed students' reactions to computers at the University of Santiago de Compostela with a number of measures including trait anxiety, computer anxiety, and experiences with computers. Their study showed a similar gender–computer anxiety relationship: females were more anxious about using computers than males. In Great Britain, Colley, Gale, and Harris (1994) surveyed students at the University of Leicester. They found that men showed lower computer anxiety, higher confidence, and more positive attitudes toward computers than did women. Similarly, Okebukola and

Woda (1993) conducted a survey of Australian high school students. Girls indicated significantly higher anxiety toward computers than boys and had generally lower interest in their use. These gender difference in anxiety and interest appeared even when Okebukola and Woda carefully matched the male and female high school student participants on other variables such as home ownership of computers, enrollment in computing classes, years of experience in using computers, as well as the respondents' socioeconomic status. Reinen and Plomp (1997) examined the data collected by the International Association for the Evaluation of Educational Achievement. The data covered numerous studies in 10 countries, including the United States. They concluded that "concern about gender equity expressed by many educational practitioners is right. Females know less about information technology, enjoy using the computer less than male students, and perceive more problems with models and activities carried out with computers in schools" (p. 65).

So, as Jared and Martha prepare for school, the proverbial cards are stacked against Martha. The research suggests that Martha will have a more difficult time than Jared with the computers in her classroom. She will probably have less *access* to a computer at home, and her interest in using it will decline. As she goes through school, she will need to find ways to combat the anxiety if she is to reap the benefits that computers can add to her life. But the problem should not be Martha's. We have a societal problem in need of a cure. Finding solutions may be easier if we can understand the causes of the gender inequity in computer anxiety. We tackle that issue in the next section.

WHY ARE THERE GENDER DIFFERENCES IN COMPUTER ANXIETY?

They Talk to You, Not to Me

Why do girls become disaffected and anxious when working with computers? There is no simple answer to this question. However, there is considerable force behind the thought that girls grow up learning that computers communicate to boys, not to them. Boys, on the other hand, grow up more comfortably with the knowledge that computers do indeed communicate with them.

Let's consider 5-year-old Martha again, embarking on her school career. Within the next few years, she will experience "games" designed to help her with her studies, games for home use, games in her friends' houses, games in shopping centers and so forth. In essence, her experience with computers will largely be a function of entertainment experiences, some of them cleverly designed for use in school as aids to the learning process.

Computer programs designed to help teach children their mathematics, language, science and social studies, known as *information technology (IT) programs* or *computer assisted instruction (CAI),* comprise a multi-billion-dollar industry. In the earlier grades, the chief benefit of such educational computer programs is purported to be the increased motivation it provides for children to learn a particular subject matter. As Mark Lepper and Tom Malone (1987) put it, the ability to "make learning fun" is a cherished attribute of computers in education.

In practice, however, learning may not be as "fun" for Martha as it will be for Jared, given the current state of IT programs that are often used in classrooms. Lepper and Malone asked students of both genders what they liked or preferred in educational computer programs.

What Boys Like; What Girls Like

Not surprisingly, boys indicated that they liked learning programs that were in a game format. They particularly liked the games that focused on sports, war, or space. They liked competition. They liked the reliance on rapid eye-hand coordination. Boys particularly liked sound effects to accompany their learning and also liked flashing lights to signify their successes. In short, boys liked the "bells and whistles" to help make their learning fun.

Girls had different preferences for educational software features. They did not appreciate war, sports, or space stories. They did not like the exploding lights and sound. They did not enjoy the eye-hand coordination (e.g., the pointing of a gun at an oncoming tank before a mathematics question could be answered) that is part and parcel of many IT experiences. To the contrary, girls preferred their IT programs to be more like learning tools. They wanted the programs to help them with their learning through direct and frequent feedback, and they preferred that this feedback be communicated in words rather than exploding icons.

An elementary school teacher, who has watched many boys and girls work with computers in her classroom, made the following observation:

> I have noticed a gender difference in how young boys differ from young girls in using the computer. Boys act out more violence on the computer than girls.... Left to their own free choice, many boys will draw bloodied people with guns and knives and then blow them up over and over again.... Girls draw hearts, flowers, and rainbows. They want their drawings saved and printed.

It should be pointed out that not every girl liked learning tools better than games, nor did every boy want to learn by blowing up battleships or landing on a faraway asteroid. On average, however, there are striking gender differences in preferences for different approaches to learning on the computer .

Features of IT Programs

Given these preferences, it would be reasonable to imagine that computer-assisted instruction would be available to match various learning styles. However, this has rarely been the case. From the beginning of computer-assisted instruction software, motivating children to learn has been wedded to the very same features of computer programs that proliferate in video arcades. We refer to the stories that these programs employ as *metaphors* because the stories serve as the basis for comparing the learning activity to a fantasy context. The metaphors used in IT programs have been overwhelmingly wedded to the preferences expressed by boys rather than girls. Who can imagine anything but the preferences that boys like in such programs as Slam Dunk Math, Word Invasion, and Space War Math?

Consider one such IT program available for classroom use entitled Demolition Division. A promotional blurb describes it as follows: "An opportunity to practice the division of problems (sic) in a war game format. Tanks move across the screen as guns from bulkheads are fired by the student as he answers the problem. Hits and misses (correct and incorrect answers) are recorded at the bottom of the screen."

This program" has it all." It has almost all of the features that Lepper and Malone found to be motivating—but for boys only. It has a war-based metaphor. It involves eye-hand coordination, as the guns must be pointed at the correct tank before the division problems can be answered. Competition is built into the program, for the entire metaphor is a competition between the tanks and the guns. Correct answers are rewarded by the tanks being blown up on the computer screen. Incorrect answers result in the destruction of the student's gun position. The hits and misses are even stored in "bunkers" at the bottom of the screen. The program "has it all." But where is the learning tool aspect of this game? Where is the verbal feedback that we know girls prefer? They are nowhere to be found.

The problem with tailoring the learning activities to preferences expressed by boys is not just that boys are more engaged or excited about the activity than are girls. We think that a more invidious, detrimental process is also occurring. Girls are learning that the computer is a learning device that is not communicating with them ... that is not interested in them. Girls are foreign to the culture of the video game qua teaching tool; they learn that they are outsiders who can witness, rather than be part of, the communication. The learning games themselves have far more characters that boys can identify with and far fewer that girls can identify with (Chappel, 1996). The same thing happens when the instructors of computer science courses (who are, by and large, males) use sports statistics and other information geared toward stereotypically male interests to illustrate problems in class. In effect, using such examples in class suggests to girls that the class is not for them.

Imagine a more overt version of this type of communication. Suppose one morning Martha arrived at school to hear her teacher say, "Today's lesson is for the boys in the class. Boys will understand what I am saying; boys will be really interested in the lesson; boys will be able to follow the lesson; boys will learn from the lesson." Then, turning to Martha and her friends, the teacher says: "Of course, girls, you may listen too. In fact, I would like it if you would try to follow my lesson. However, I do not expect that you will be interested, I do not expect you to be able to follow very well, and I do not expect you to learn very much."

In most jurisdictions, such an outrageous instruction would lead to disciplinary action against the teacher. However, we are arguing that, in its own subtle way, this is precisely what computers do when they function as teaching machines, when they teach via IT programs such as Demolition Division. What would we expect would be the result of such a communication from the instructor? It would not be surprising to find that children who receive the message that the instruction is not for them would feel alienated, have a lowered sense of self-efficacy, and would feel pessimistic about their being able to perform the learning tasks adequately. If they were asked to use the computer in their classroom, it is understandable that they would suffer considerable anxiety, discomfort and stress. It would also not be surprising to find that the children had negative attitudes toward the computer and computer use. That seems to be the situation in which girls find themselves as they move through the current educational system.

COMPUTER ANXIETY AND ITS RELATION
TO THE FEATURES OF IT SOFTWARE

Joan Hall, Chuck Huff, and I conducted a study to examine whether the motivational embellishments that IT programs employ to motivate students to learn also influence the degree of anxiety girls and boys feel when using the software (Cooper, Hall, & Huff, 1990). In order to test our hypothesis, we conducted a study with children from a middle school in New Jersey. We argued that math instruction programs that used predominantly male-preferred features, such as Demolition Division and Slam Dunk Math, would create anxiety for girls as they attempt to learn their mathematics from what are supposedly motivational programs. On the other hand, we speculated that girls would *not* experience computer anxiety if they learned their mathematics from an IT program that contained the formal features that girls more typically like. Recall from the work by Malone and Lepper that girls prefer IT software that functions as a learning tool and is characterized by straightforward lessons, with frequent feedback in verbal form. Explosions, lights, bells, and whistles are not part of such programs, nor are competitive, rapid-fire responses or eye-hand coordination exercises. Metaphors in the form of war, sports, and space also play no role in such programs.

In our study we examined how students performed and how they felt after using two types of IT programs—one that had the formal features preferred by males, and one that had the formal features preferred by females. One program we used in this study was the previously mentioned Demolition Division. The other was Arithmetic Classroom: Fractions. Finding examples of programs containing the formal features that boys enjoy was no problem at all. They can be found quite readily from software publishers and from the shelves of many school systems' available IT software. Finding examples of programs that feature direct feedback learning tools in the absence of aggressive or sports-oriented metaphors proved a more difficult undertaking.

Arithmetic Classroom: Fractions is a good example of software containing the formal features preferred by girls. The program is designed to teach students how to divide and multiply fractions. Its deeper goal is to have students understand that fractions are instances of the division of two numbers. The way the program goes about its teaching is illustrated in Fig. 2.1.

After politely obtaining the student's name, the program has the student work through examples of multiplying and dividing fractions. It then presents sample problems to the student. If the student obtains the correct answer, the program congratulates the students (verbally!), and presents a new problem. If the student is incorrect, then the program informs the student that it is incorrect and offers instruction about how to solve the problem. The process continues until the problem is solved correctly. If the student does not get the correct answer after three attempts to correct the student's error, the program presents a new and easier version of the problem. The formal features of the program contain no games, no lights, no sound, and no competition. The lesson and the feedback are conveyed in clear language.

Contrast this approach to the manufacturer's description of Demolition Division. You can note that in the description of that program, the noun *student* is replaced by the pronoun *he*. There is clearly little thought that the student who is presumably going to be motivated learn about division from this program might actually be a girl.

FIG. 2.1.   An illustration of the teaching method of Arithmetic Classroom as it appears on the computer screen.

In Demolition Division, students are presented with a series of five division problems simultaneously. As Fig. 2.2 illustrates, the problems are presented in pictorial display of military tanks. The student controls the artillery battery. The student's task is to aim the artillery at the appropriate tank, thus signifying which problem he or she intends to answer. Simultaneously, all tanks are proceeding toward the artillery. If the student successfully answers the problem toward which his or her gun is pointed, the tank explodes on the screen. Quickly, the student can point to another problem, attempt to answer that one, and move to the next. If any of the five tanks reaches the student's artillery battery before all of the questions are answered, the enemy "wins," the student's position explodes, and a new screen full of problems appears on the computer monitor.

The formal features of this program involve aggressive war metaphors, eye-hand coordination, competition, explosions, and so forth—many of the formal features that boys enjoy and girls do not. It is easy to think of Demolition Division as a video game rather than a learning device. However, it is important to remember that it is not designed as a game to play at the video arcade in the local mall but rather as a device to teach division in the classroom. Its problems are carefully chosen, its visual display provides feedback for correct and incorrect problems, and students are encour-

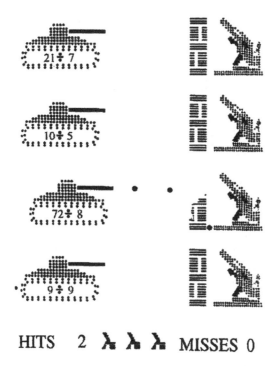

HITS   2 ⋏ ⋏ ⋏ MISSES 0

FIG. 2.2.   An illustration of the teaching method of Demolition Division as it appears on the computer screen.

aged to do simple division quickly and accurately. The program designers went about the instruction, however, in a way that captures precisely the features that appear to motivate boys.

Hall, Huff, and I reasoned that trying to learn division by using Demolition Division would arouse computer anxiety in girls. In contrast, we reasoned that boys would be comfortable with the motivational embellishments used in Demolition Division. They might enjoy learning arithmetic in this way and should not experience computer anxiety. Our prediction was reversed for Arithmetic Classroom: Fractions. We suggested that boys would not feel comfortable working with computer-generated graphics that contained verbal feedback for correct and incorrect answers and that contained none of the space, war, or sports metaphors to which they were accustomed. By contrast, we thought the Arithmetic Classroom approach to learning would be experienced with greater comfort by girls. We predicted that boys would experience more anxiety than girls when working with the Arithmetic Classroom IT program.

One day, when they came to class, sixth-grade children were asked to take a brief pre-test of their ability at division. After that, they were taken to the school's computer center, a rather large room that contained a number of computer stations. The students were given instruction about operating the software on their computers and then allowed to spend 30 minutes working with their computer program. Half of the students had Demolition Division loaded on the computer. The other half had Arithmetic Classroom: Fractions. In order for the students not to be overly curious about having their fellow students working with a different program that might be making different sounds and displaying a different visual presentation on the screen, all of the students in the computer center at any one time learned from the same program. Thus, if a student was assigned to the computer center at, for example, 10:00 A.M., that student—and all of the others assigned to the center at 10:00 A.M.—would learn arithmetic with Demolition Division. All students who came to the computer center at 10:30 learned with Arithmetic Classroom. Each student came to the computer center only once and thus was either in the condition in which the IT formal features were what males enjoy (Demolition Division) or the condition in which the formal features of the IT software were what girls enjoy (Arithmetic Classroom).

After working with the program to which they were assigned, the students recorded their degree of anxiety. They did this on a self-report scale adapted from the well-used scale developed by Mattson (1960). The students also answered a series of questions that assessed their attitudes toward computers in general and toward the specific task on which they had worked during the morning's activity. Finally, the students returned to their classroom, where they took another test assessing their facility with fractions and division. Of course, it is also important to measure whether any learning took place after working with the IT programs and how learning related to computer anxiety.

Remember our predictions: We expected that girls who learned division with Demolition Division would experience more anxiety than boys learning with the same program. Conversely, boys learning with Arithmetic Classroom were predicted to experience more anxiety than girls.

The results supported this prediction. Figure 2.3 presents the data. The higher the number that is reported, the greater the amount of anxiety. First, note that the Demolition Division program caused all students to experience greater anxiety than Arithmetic Classroom. That is undoubtedly because its quick, competitive format resulted in stress for all players. Nonetheless, the girls who worked with the Demolition Division program experienced significantly more anxiety (mean = 77.01) than the boys (mean = 55.94). Examining the results from Arithmetic Classroom, the program with the formal features preferred by girls, we see the opposite pattern. Boys experienced more anxiety (mean = 28.23) after working with the program employing features that girls prefer than did the girls

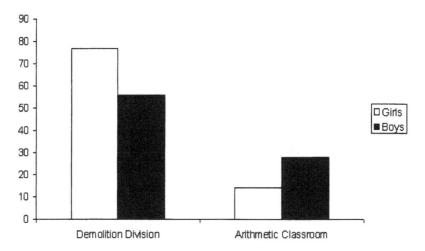

FIG. 2.3. Reported anxiety after working with gender-typed CAI program. Adapted from Cooper, Hall, & Huff, 1990, *Personality and Social Psychology Bulletin, 16*, pp. 419–429. Copyright © 1990 by Sage Publications, Inc. Adapted with permission of Sage Publications.

(mean = 13.7). This pattern resulted in a significant statistical interaction ($p < .05$).

The results of the post-test of arithmetic ability did not show much change, perhaps because of the brief exposure to the IT software. However, it is important to note from an educational perspective that there was a significant negative correlation between performance and anxiety ($p < .05$). The more anxiety a student experienced with the IT program, the worse his or her performance was on the math problems. Therefore, creating anxiety for an individual student was related to that student learning less of the arithmetic lesson.

What lessons can we take from these data? First, the formal features of the IT program with which a student works makes a crucial difference to his or her level of anxiety. Heightened anxiety is related to working with software that appears to be designed for the opposite gender. Second, academic performance is correlated with anxiety such that the greater the anxiety, the worse the performance. The results show very clearly that it is a mistake to require girls to learn from educational computer software that has the formal features that are perceived to be the province of boys and, conversely, a mistake to require boys to learn from software that has the features that are seen as the province of girls.

In England, a group of investigators had a similar idea. Littleton, Light, Joiner, Messer, and Barnes (1998) reasoned that one of the difficulties girls have with learning from IT programs is that the characters in the program are not appealing to them. A previous study had followed boys and girls as they tried to master a program called King and Crown. The program involved complex cognitive tasks including mapping and spatial relations. The prior study (Barbierri & Light, 1992) had found that boys did better on the program than girls: They learned faster, enjoyed it more, and had more positive attitudes. Littleton et al. noted that the adventure game format required learners to identify with warriors in the context of an adventure game. They reasoned that the lack of identification with the characters may have caused the girls in the class to experience greater computer anxiety, lack of interest, and poorer performance. To test this, the Littleton group ran an experiment. They located a computer program that taught the same skills as King and Crown but used characters that the 11-year-old girls could identify with. The program presented the same problems and called for identical mapping and spatial solutions. This time, both genders were successful. Of course, boys had been successful on the King and Crown task. Forty-six percent had solved the tasks completely, and the same percentage were successful on the gender-neutral version. For girls, fewer than 8% reached the solution when the task was embedded in the King and Crown format, but more than 50% solved the task completely when it was in the gender-neutral format.

There is clearly an educational problem implied by these data. We have seen that girls can do very well on educational computer software that is designed with formal features and characters that girls can appreciate. But they do poorly, experience anxiety, and have negative attitudes toward computers if the software has characters they do not identify with or has formal features that are incompatible with their interests. Each gender can suffer if the program is written to capture the features preferred by the other gender. However, as Chappel (1996) has reported, in the real world of education and business, programs overwhelmingly favor male interests and male identification. Although there have been some laudable im-

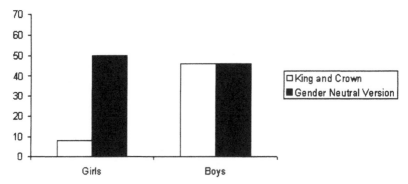

FIG. 2.4.   Percentage of children solving the task as a function of type of program Adapted from Littleton et al., 1998, Gender, task scenarios and children's computer-based problem solving. *Educational Psychology, 18,* pp. 327–340, copyright © 1998 by Taylor and Francis LTD. Adapted by permission.

provements in recent years, the persistence of male-oriented software in the educational market is still substantial. Until software is more readily available that is either gender-neutral or more suited to the preferences expressed by girls, the problem of computer anxiety will continue to be borne by females. Girls will experience it more than boys; women will grow up feeling anxious about computers and be more reluctant than men to interact with computers. In a society that is becoming more and more reliant on the ability to use computers, this may have far-reaching consequences for professional employment and satisfaction.

GENDER INEQUITY IN THE OLDER GRADES

Computer anxiety for girls does not go away with age or decline with more schooling. To the contrary, it seems to be exacerbated with time. One of the reasons the inequities increase with time is that as girls shun the computer and boys gravitate toward it, not only do boys become more comfortable learning computer software, but also the culture that builds up around the computer becomes extremely male oriented.

Janet Schofield (1995) studied computer education at "Whitmore High School," a fictitiously named but very real institution serving a major urban center. The school had established a computer center where interested students could come to use the computer during their lunch hour. Although the school's population was approximately equally divided between male and female and between White and African American, Schofield described the computer center as a "White boys' club." The club was well attended by Caucasian males, but very rarely by females or by African American males.

Schofield found that boys came to the computer center because they enjoyed using the software, they enjoyed the competition, and they enjoyed the sense of mastery they experienced when they were the highest scorer on a game or when they figured out how to solve a particular problem. The boys at the center became a social club, ostracizing those of a different race or gender.

In contrast, girls did not find the need or interest to break into this club that had as its basis the use of computers. When Schofield asked the girls at the school what they disliked about the computer room, they reported that they found the room noisy and distracting and that it was difficult to get work done in that environment. Interestingly, none of the boys mentioned any of these factors. Recall that, earlier in this chapter, we examined Lepper and Malone's findings about what girls liked about computer programs and saw that, first and foremost, girls wanted computers to serve as "learning tools." That is, they wanted the computer to help them efficiently with specific tasks. Consistent with this finding, Schofield's interviewers asked the high school students at Whitmore what motivated them to come to the computer room. All of the girls interviewed mentioned task-related motivations, whereas fewer than 15% of the boys mentioned such reasons.

From our review of the psychological literature, it seems to us that the introduction of computers as competitive, game-oriented learning rather than problem-focused, task-oriented learning begins a process of alienation and anxiety that many girls experience throughout their school years. The attraction that boys have for the computer not only ends up giving them greater experience, greater confidence, and greater comfort, it also establishes the social milieu that surrounds computers as one that is oriented toward males. Such was the "White boys' club" that Schofield observed at Whitmore.

Schofield's observations at Whitmore reveal that the differential access to computers transcends the voluntary "club" aspect of computing to pervade the classroom at the high school level. In the 2 years that Schofield's team studied Whitmore High, the number of boys who enrolled in the basic computer science course exceeded the number of girls who enrolled, 54% to 46%. Importantly, this inequity became far greater in the advanced computer science courses. In the advanced computer science courses, the ratio of male students to female students was a shockingly unequal 80% to 20%, a 4-to-1 ratio.

Partly because boys form the overwhelming majority of the students in the computer classes, and partly because the overwhelming majority of computer teachers tend to be male, many of the examples used in classrooms tend to be correlated with male interests. Schofield noted that, at Whitmore High, sports statistics were often used to provide the data for computer analyses. Not just any sports—almost always, the sports were those traditionally associated with males, such as NFL Football. This creates a compound anxiety for many girls. As we have seen earlier in this chapter, girls have gone through their primary school years learning that the computer is a learning device primarily intended for boys. They also learn that the culture, in voluntary activities as well as the classroom, is a culture that is dominated by male interests. The male-oriented nature of the culture simultaneously reinforces the notion that computing activities are directed solely to males and arouses its own anxiety by forcing girls into the role of the out-group trying to cope within the rule system and communication pattern of another group.

Schofield (1995) writes about Denise, one of only four girls in an advanced computer science class:

> Denise ... starts to work on her computer program which is similar to everyone else's since it deals with football [statistics]. Doug laughs at Denise's

program because he notices that some of the ... teams ... [she listed] were not football teams like the Red Sox. He laughs because she does not know which of the teams are football teams and which are not.

Denise is typical of so many students in so many schools. Ridicule from trying to cope with boys' cultural knowledge adds to the feeling of computer anxiety to make it far less likely that she will ever enjoy working with computers.

THE CHILDREN GROW UP: ON TO UNIVERSITY

The research we have examined thus far suggests that the seeds of computer anxiety are sown early in the school years but continue to have consequences as children develop. When girls receive the message that computer lessons are communications not intended for them, it has far-reaching and long-lasting consequences. Girls not only prefer to avoid the computer and experience anxiety when they must interact with it, they often conclude that they do not have the competence to use it. We can say that girls acquire a diminished sense of *self-efficacy* about computers. They feel that they are not as competent to use computers as boys are. This feeling takes many forms, including the often-expressed belief that many girls have that they will break the computer, or ruin the software during their time on the computer.

Janet Schofield's research provided an insight into the problems that adolescent females have of gaining access to, and feeling comfortable about, using computers in their schools. When boys and girls become college men and women, do the differences in efficacy and anxiety remain? We know that, by the end of high school, more males have had computer courses, are more likely to have learned programming languages, and are more likely to report having computers in their homes (Selwyn, 1998). Research is now converging on the conclusion that computer anxiety and loss of self-efficacy do not disappear as the elementary school children move toward adulthood. Research from the United States and many other countries shows that even among the highly selected group of young adults who continue on to college, computer anxiety and the sense of efficacy are inequitable across gender.

In a companion study to our survey of elementary school children discussed earlier, Gita Wilder, Diane Mackie, and I also conducted a survey of newly enrolled men and women at Princeton University (Wilder et al., 1985). We suspected that among this group of students, differences between the genders in computer experience would be diminished. We were correct about this suspicion. About half of the men and half of the women had taken computer courses in high school. There were no significant differences in the number of programming languages they knew, and there were no significant differences in the percentage of students of each gender who reported having a computer at home. Unlike the younger children surveyed, both males and females in the university group indicated that they thought that computers were equally appropriate for both genders.

On the surface, it would seem that, among the highly selected student population, differences in feelings about the computer would not be a function of gender. When digging deeper, such a conclusion was found to be untrue. Despite the similarity of their experiences with computers and their similar knowledge of computer languages, deep underlying differences remained. When asked how comfortable they were using the computer, there was an overwhelming gender effect. On a scale in which 31 expressed extreme comfort and 1 expressed extreme discomfort, males expressed a mean of 22.8 while the mean for females was 18.8 ($p < .0001$). When asked how they *felt about* their level of computer skills, women indicated far less feelings of competence (mean = 7.96) than their male counterparts (mean = 11.54)—this difference occurring despite the fact that their computer skills and experience were not objectively different.

Wilder, Mackie, and I examined the data a bit more closely. Recall that not every student had taken computer courses or learned programming languages. We divided the males and females between those who had computer experience and those who had none. The feelings of discomfort and confidence ran so deep that females who had computer experience rated themselves as *less* comfortable than did the males who had absolutely no high school computing experience. The men with no secondary school computer experience whatsoever rated themselves as highly on their skill with computers as did the women who had considerable experience. Thus, even among a group of students who were highly selected for college admission and whose overall skill and experience with computers was objectively similar, women still expressed the belief that they did not have the skill or the comfort to use computers effectively.

Changing Times

When Bob Dylan wrote, "The times, they are a changin'," he envisioned a society that becomes more fair, equitable, and wise over time. It evolves to recognize its social problems and overcome them. Seventeen years after the publication of Wilder et al.'s (1985) survey, we returned to the Princeton University campus to see whether times had changed. Had the passage of time alleviated the digital divide for women? We found that it had not.

The Princeton University freshmen in our sample were highly qualified academically. The women surveyed had extremely high mathematics preparation, with 80% having studied calculus in high school. How did they feel about computers? We asked the students to report how comfortable they felt with computers on a 7-point scale. The results, shown in Fig. 2.5, tell the same story that we found 17 years ago. Freshmen males were considerably more comfortable with computers than were freshman women.

While at college, students will not only learn about computers but, like Jared and Martha in elementary school, they will also be using computers to learn additional skills. For example, when they enroll in social science courses, from economics to psychology, they will need to learn statistical inference. We asked students to imagine that they were enrolled in a psychology statistics course. In the class, the professor asked them to use a computer program to complete a statistics assignment. We asked them how comfortable they would imagine themselves feeling in the statistics class when using the computer program. Remember that the women were experienced and competent in mathematics. In fact, these particular freshmen women had more advanced preparation in high school mathematics than did their male counterparts. Nonetheless, the data showed that women expected to feel less comfortable doing their statistics assignment on the computer than did males (see Fig. 2.6). The discomfort the students felt about computers transferred to the psychology class and caused women to anticipate greater discomfort in that subject as well. Just as we worried that Martha would come to dislike many of her subjects if they were taught on computers, Princeton University women expressed concerns about their other subjects if working with IT programs was an integral component.

One of the reasons that our male incoming freshmen may feel more comfortable with computers than the female students is previous com-

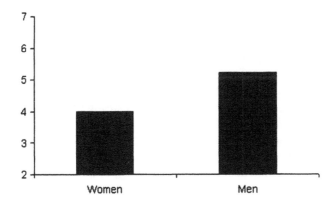

FIG. 2.5.   Princeton University freshmen 2002: Reported comfort with computers in general.

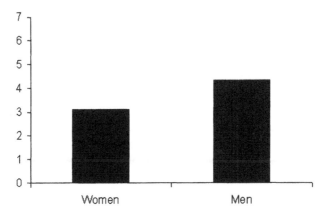

FIG. 2.6. Reported comfort using computers to complete statistics assignment for psychology class.

puter experience. Our survey showed that this was so. Every male student we surveyed (100%) reported having some sort of formal instruction in computers, ranging from formal programming courses to courses in word processing and document formatting. In contrast, far fewer of the females reported having previous formal instruction in computers (55%).

We wondered if students' previous computer experience would influence their reported feelings of comfort when using the computerized statistics program discussed earlier. Results from this analysis were very informative. The group of young women with some type of formal computer instruction in high school reported *more* comfort when imagining learning the program for their psychology assignment ($M = 3.4$) than those young women who had no formal computer instruction in high school ($M = 2.8$). Even though none of the young women had experience with the statistical software itself, their computer experience had made them more comfortable with computers in general. This comfort then generalized to other sorts of computer programs.

These findings highlight the importance of prior experience with computers. From these results, we think there is strong reason to believe that young women's failure to take computer courses in high school will lead them to be behind in the college courses of today's world. Whether they plan to major in computer science or instead in one of the social sciences like economics, political science, psychology, or sociology, it is essential that young women and men alike arrive at the university of their choice with some experience and comfort with computers.

The times have not yet changed.

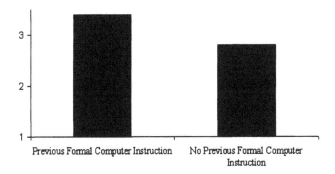

FIG. 2.7 Female students' feelings of comfort with program depending on previous formal computer instruction.

LEARNING STYLES, PROGRAMMING STYLES, AND COMMUNICATION

In colleges and universities around the world, far fewer women enroll in computer science courses than men. As a result, many more men than women have training and expertise to write computer programs. This may exacerbate the gender bias that exists in educational software. But there may be other factors that discourage women scholars from pursuing computer programming in college. In this section, we discuss research that has been conducted on computer programming styles. In particular, work shows that men and women tend to prefer to program in different styles, and that the style that is taught in the vast majority of classes is that which is preferred by men. We think that in order for people to feel part of a group or culture, it is important for them to feel like they belong or fit in. Perceptions of "belongingness" can come about in several different ways. People are more likely to feel as if they belong to a group to the degree that they are similar to and have things in common with other group members. An individual will feel as if he or she belongs to a group to the degree that the other group members "speak the same language."

Sherry Turkle and Seymour Papert (1990), researchers at MIT, made extensive observations and conducted personal interviews with male and female students taking computer programming courses. Through their observations and interviews, Turkle and Papert discovered that students tended to take one of two basic approaches to programming.

One programming approach, referred to as the "formal" style by Turkle and Papert (1990), is the method that is both the most widely accepted and most commonly taught as the "correct" way to program. The formal style is rule-driven and hierarchical. Programming done in this style tends to be modular—programmers with a formal approach start with a vision or plan for a program and then work on separate units to achieve a program that meets the original vision. In this sense it is a "top-down" approach. Turkle and Papert liken the formal style to computer programming to a writing style that begins with a formal outline.

In contrast to the canonical, formal style, Turkle and Papert also observed that a significant proportion of the students in their research tended to use and prefer another style of programming, an approach they refer to as "concrete." In contrast to the "top-down" style of formal programming, concrete programming is characterized by a "bottom-up" style. Programmers using the concrete method tend to start with the basic units and work creatively to form an end product. Turkle and Papert draw an analogy between this style and other creative endeavors such as painting or making a collage. The final product ends up being a synthesis of the parts, rather than an a priori planned product achieved through development of the parts.

Because formal programming is considered to be the correct approach among teachers of programming classes, often students who tend toward a more concrete approach are discouraged from following their natural tendencies and instead are encouraged to adopt the formal approach. The main reason this research is relevant to us here is because Turkle and Papert showed that the different programming styles were rather strongly correlated with the gender of the students. Although there were some males and females that preferred to program in the formal style and the concrete style, their observations and interviews indicated that females were much more likely than males to tend toward concrete approaches to programming, whereas overall, males appeared to prefer the more formal, rule-driven programming style.

Turkle and Papert make a compelling argument and report evidence from interviews that when girls who prefer a concrete programming approach are "forced" by their programming teachers to adopt the more formal style, they become alienated from programming. One consequence of this alienation is that they come to view the computer less as an interesting opportunity to be creative, and more as a tool, or a means to an end to develop a program. As a consequence of this alienation, or boredom, girls tend to not pursue programming as much as they might had they been allowed to exercise their initial concrete tendencies and program creatively.

It is important to point out that research has shown that the formal and the concrete programming styles can both lead to equivalently sophisticated final products. For this reason, Turkle and Papert argue that there are no objective reasons why teachers should dissuade students from utilizing traditional approaches. Through data obtained in interviews, then, it appears that one reason girls become disillusioned with computer programming is that, in one sense, the classes that they are taking are being taught in such a way that they do not "speak to them" in the language with which they feel the most comfortable. As a consequence, girls become alienated from programming and begin to focus on topics of study that allow them to use the intellectual styles with which they are the most comfortable.

It is not only girls who suffer as a consequence of not being able to exercise their true capabilities in the computer science classroom. It is also likely that programmers and the computer industry as a whole are missing out on potential innovations that would arise from a population of programmers whose natural tendency is to program in a more bottom-up, spontaneous, and arguably more creative way. There is much to be gained for both women and the computer field as a whole by acknowledging that there are different intellectual styles and programming approaches and encouraging programming that adopts both.

BIOLOGICAL SEX AND PSYCHOLOGICAL GENDER: "GETTING WITH THE PROGRAM" FOR YOUR GENDER

Very few of us believe that there is a gene for computer anxiety. Yet, we see the marked impact that being a boy or being girl makes in the way in which people react to computers in their schools. The roots of computer anxiety are many. We discuss several of them in this book. Anxiety leads to a negative attitude that, in turn, leads to reluctance to use computers. Parents, teachers, and other adult socializers in the child's world all have their roles to play. At this point, however, we wish to emphasize the enormous importance of the social construction of gender. We learn from an early age what it means to be a boy or a girl. Young children may not know the biological significance of sexual organs and reproduction, but they learn quickly about the roles, norms, and obligations that are contingent upon their biology. We refer to these as *psychological gender*.

In his highly influential theory of child development, Laurence Kohlberg (1966) suggested that children, before the age of 5 or 6, do not have a sense of the permanence of their maleness or femaleness. Although they acquire the ability to label themselves as boys or girls beginning at an early age (Thompson, 1975), it is only later that they realize the permanence and inevitability of their status as boys or girls. The transition between knowing the label and recognizing its permanence is called the stage of *gender constancy*. If you ask a boy who has not reached this stage if he will be a boy or a girl if he wears a dress, he is very likely to tell you that he will be a girl. And, of course, the same transitory attribution works for a girl. Wearing daddy's business suit likely will convince Martha that she is a boy.

Such naiveté disappears at the stage of gender constancy. Boys are boys; girls are girls; it will always be so. But along with the notion that gender is permanent comes a desire to know what boys do and what girls do. What are the social behaviors that go along with this ever-present and permanent distinction? It is at this point that girls and boys become motivated to learn the dos and don'ts of their gender (Frey & Ruble, 1992). The stereotypes associated with gender now come in to play. Should I play with my Tonka truck or my dress-up doll? Should I be more interested in baseball or dance? There is information to be gathered. Parents, peers, and teachers provide many of the answers. So, too, do popular media that include cartoon shows, advertisements, and MTV. Children will differ in how much information they gather for their understanding of appropriate gender attitudes, feelings, and behaviors. Some parents may communicate a rather large set of prescriptions and proscriptions about what it means to be a boy or girl. Other parents may present a smaller and more flexible set of standards.

Len Newman, Diane Ruble, and I investigated computer attitudes among young children who were close to reaching, or who had just reached, the stage of gender constancy (Newman, Ruble, & Cooper, 1995). We tested more than 200 young elementary school children in a suburban school district near New York City. Gender constancy was measured by a scale developed by Slaby and Frey (1975) and modified by Frey and Ruble (1992). The scale consisted of 14 not-very-subtle items that included:

- Could you be a (OPPOSITE-GENDER CHILD) if you wanted to be?
- If you played games that (OPPOSITE-GENDER CHILDREN) usually play, would you then really be a boy or really be a girl?
- (for girls): If you were strong and played football, would you be a boy?
- (for boys): If you were gentle and cooked dinner, would you be a girl?

Children were also asked about their knowledge of gender stereotypes. That is, they were read a series of activities and roles, and asked if such activities were usually carried out by males or females. These included social behaviors ("runs away from scary places," "brags a lot") and roles such as nurse, doctor, and secretary. We thought that the psychological nature of gender would lead to the following prediction: Children who had reached the stage of gender constancy and whose knowledge of social stereotypes was the most complete would be the group of children who would show stereotypical computer attitudes. We thought that girls who knew the content of stereotypes in other realms, such as the social behaviors and roles just described, would have the most negative attitudes toward computers—provided they had reached the stage of gender constancy. Conversely, boys who were gender constant and who had a full knowledge of social stereotypes would be the ones chomping at the pro-verbial bit to approach, play with, and use computers.

The results supported our predictions. Girls who were highly knowl-edgeable of gender stereotypes professed far less positive attitudes to-ward computers, if and only if they were at the stage of gender constancy. This machine, which was quite popular for all children prior to the stage of gender constancy, had already lost its appeal for the gender constant girls knowledgeable of the stereotype. One of the truly vulnerable periods, then, that gives rise to negative attitudes for girls is the stage in their lives during which they are developing gender constancy. It is then that they so-cially construct what is appropriate for their gender and it is then that they are motivated to assess the stereotypes—the dos and don'ts of being a girl. It is then that they are at risk of inferring that it is inappropriate for them to be interested in this stereotypically male activity.

Brosnan (1998) made yet another prediction about the relationship of psychological gender to computer attitudes. Brosnan noted that children, like adults, differ in the degree to which they are characterized by mascu-line and/or feminine interests. Some boys have orientations toward their social world that can be characterized as highly masculine, some as more feminine, and some as androgynous (high on both masculine and femi-nine interests.) Similarly, girls can be highly feminine, masculine, or an-drogynous. Brosnan suggested that attitudes toward computers and IT would be predicted by a child's gender role orientation. That is, more than biological sex, children's attitudes toward technology would be a function of their gender role orientation. In Brosnan's research, children in a Lon-don elementary school were administered a test of gender role identifica-tion. Test items that measured masculine identity asked to agree or disagree with statements such as, "I am good at taking charge of things," and "I am a leader among my friends." Feminine gender role identity was assessed with items such as "I am a gentle person," and "I can tell when someone needs help."

Brosnan's study shed more light on the psychological mechanisms that contribute to the relationship of gender and computer attitudes. His data again confirmed the relationship we have discussed previously—that is, boys have more positive attitudes about computers than girls. More inter-estingly, however, Brosnan also found that the masculine and feminine in-terests that characterize children's psychological orientation predicted computer attitudes, independent of the biological sex of the child. Boys who had more masculine gender role identities also had more positive feelings about IT and what they could accomplish on computers than did boys with less masculine identity. Similarly, girls with more feminine gen-der role orientations had more negative attitudes toward computers than girls with less feminine identities. The overall correlations with masculinity and femininity scores were highly significant, independent of the biological sex of the children.

CONSEQUENCES OF COMPUTER ANXIETY: COMPUTER AVOIDANCE AND DISIDENTIFICATION

Computer anxiety leads girls to avoid computers. Girls are less likely to have computers in their homes (Selwyn, 1998). And even if we consider only those homes in which boys and girls have access to computers, boys report using their computers more often than do girls. Compared to boys, girls avoid activities that focus on computers. Consider video arcades or the market for computer games (Selwyn, 1998). Anyone who has even glanced inside a video arcade or gone into a store that sells computer games knows that they are overwhelmingly populated by boys. One study that observed activity at a video arcade over the course of several weeks placed the boy:girl ratio in video arcades at 11:1 (Cooper, 1991). Neil Selwyn surveyed nearly 1,000 high school students in Great Britain. One of the high school students (a boy) interviewed by Selwyn summed it up well: "It's the games. Most of them are aimed at boys and that's how most people get into computers, through games ... we used them more when we were young. That's where all the games were and the girls like didn't want to know" (p. 222).

The impact of the differential levels of anxiety, the more negative attitudes and the lowered feelings of efficacy is that girls tend to shun activities that involve the computer. Some of those activities, like courses and camp experiences, have the potential to increase girls' knowledge and experience with computers. However, anxiety and negative attitudes cause girls to avoid such situations.

In the survey that we conducted in the public schools of Princeton, New Jersey, children were asked about their attitudes toward computers (Wilder et al., 1985). Consistently throughout the school years, girls had more negative attitudes than boys about computers. In addition, the children were asked to indicate if using the computer was something that "is mostly for males, mostly for females or something that is as much for one as for the other." Both males and females believed that the computer was "mostly for males." These results were replicated in a study conducted in 1997 with a group of high school students in three areas in the United States. In addition, results from a survey showed that 50% of both males and females expressed that they thought computer science was "geared toward men" (AAUW, 2000).

INTO ADULT LIFE: COMPUTERS IN THE WORKPLACE

It should not be surprising to find disparities by gender in information technology employment. As we documented in chapter 1, only 20% of young people entering IT professions are women. In many ways, the disparity began as soon as the Marthas and the Jareds of our society initiated their interaction with computer programs in their homes, their schools, or the video arcades. As we noted, by the time students declare their major field of study in college, the choice of computer science and related IT fields is 72% male. At the PhD level, it is 82% male. It is safe to say that the field of information technology, which many observers believe is the key to the higher paying and higher status positions in the 21st century, is closing rapidly to the female gender.

The situation is actually more alarming than that. If we examine what happens to people within computer-related work environments, we find that most women who do make it into IT positions do not fare very well there. Recent studies have all confirmed that women are paid less than men for doing similar work (Panteli et al., 2001), even when controlling for age, education, and experience (Baroudi & Igbaria, 1995; Wright & Jacobs, 1994; Klawe & Leveson, 1995). Furthermore, the longer people remain in their careers, the greater the disparity becomes. Men move up in salary and status; women do not.

Panteli et al. (2001) conducted an in-depth study of four companies in the United Kingdom. Consistent with the data collected in the United States and Europe (Tijdens, 1997), Panteli et al. found that women were markedly underrepresented at the higher levels of information technology departments and markedly overrepresented at the lower levels. Relative to their proportion in the IT workforce, very few women were in the management categories. For those women who were in management, most were in the customer service or support fields, whereas management in the higher status fields of hardware, systems, and software design was almost exclusively male. Overall, women were much more likely to appear in categories such as "help desk assistant" and "junior administrator." And pay? The proportion of men earning more than £40,000 was double the proportion of females. Thus, even among the small group of women who emerge from their universities still wanting to take positions in information technology fields, it is most probable that they will be found in lower status and lower paying positions than their male counterparts.

It is not only the training, pay, and access to jobs that make the IT workplace difficult for women. Panteli and her colleagues' systematic observations led them to conclude that the culture of the IT workplace is decidedly masculine. From the conversations at the water cooler to the interaction between and within gender groups, the culture is one that makes men feel comfortable and women feel uncomfortable. Hemenway (1995) observed that women who have traditional feminine work styles (for example, seeking consensus and team effort) are seen as less confident and capable than men. The "Catch-22," of course, is that women who do act in stereotypically masculine styles are disliked. They are seen as pushy and aggressive, and are ostracized by both their male and female colleagues (see also Rudman & Glick, 1999).

One woman employee at an IT company told Panteli and her colleagues, "They weren't interested in what I had to say. They [the men] were all in a clique. They wouldn't let me show them how to work anything, because I was a female." From their interviews and observations, Panteli et al. concluded, "This new and growing industry has become gendered. The growth in IT should have opened up new possibilities for women to enter these fields. However, its growth so far has been used to construct and maintain gender differences and to sustain male hierarchies" (p. 15).

It is not necessary to subscribe to the notion of an evil conspiracy, denying employment and advancement to women in IT professions. Rather, we see the "genderization" of the IT profession to be an outgrowth of the cycle that begins in childhood. Different experiences with computers from the earliest of ages generates the belief that computers are a male domain. The ensuing anxiety and negative attitudes that characterize girls' future interactions with computers only confirms that notion. The process continues through higher education and is then reinforced in the workplace, even for the small number of women who maintained their interest in IT throughout their education.

A CONCLUDING COMMENT

For most people, the computer is only a tool to help them in the pursuit of a goal. In educational environments, the computer can provide extra help to gain mastery of a field of study. It can provide motivation and expertise that supplement traditional learning tools. The use of tools to supplement education is not new; most of us can remember the use of filmstrips, videotapes, or even field trips to help motivate us and inform us as we proceeded through school. Some of us found these embellishments useful; others did not. Some of us found them fun; others did not.

The computer is special among the innovations in the educational arena because of its power and pervasiveness. Jared and Martha will interact with computers in their classroom from their first day of kindergarten until they have finished their formal education. They will play games on them; they will learn spelling, math, and grammar. They will eventually compose their papers and theses on them. If, as a society, we allow the likelihood to be higher that Martha will experience more computer anxiety than Jared, then we will have created an unacceptable inequity in the educational process, leading to even greater inequities in fields of employment.

It does not have to be so. The research presented in this chapter points to one direction for change. By considering the pervasive male-oriented metaphors that exist on educational software, we may be able to correct the educational disparity from an early age. But our understanding is far from complete. We have addressed the existence of gender inequity in computing and have presented at least one explanation for why differences exist between boys' and girls' computer anxiety. We now turn to the question of *where* children compute. In the next chapter we concentrate on the fascinating dilemma posed by the social context of educational computing.

3

The Social Context of Computing

One of the most important lessons we have learned through a century of psychological research is that people's behavior, attitudes, and thoughts are impacted dramatically by the social context. To illustrate this point, we begin this chapter with a notorious incident that occurred many years ago in New York City. The incident and its aftermath led to a fascinating social psychological experiment that vividly drives home the important point: the social context matters. It shows how the simple presence of other people impacts a person's behavior in dramatic and consequential ways. In 1964, a woman named Kitty Genovese was attacked and stabbed multiple times over a 45-minute period on the street beneath her New York City apartment by an assailant with a knife. Investigations following her death indicated that although at least 38 people living in the apartment complex had either witnessed part of the attack or heard her screams and pleas for help, not one of them attempted to intervene or even call the police for assistance (A. M. Rosenthal, 1964). Newspaper coverage following the case attributed the indifference of the neighbors to the fact that they were apathetic New Yorkers, desensitized to violence. A social psychological study conducted after the Kitty Genovese attack, however, showed that the unresponsiveness of the neighbors may have been due not to apathy, but rather, in a sad twist of fate, to the fact that there were so many of them witnessing the attack.

Following the Kitty Genovese murder, John Darley and Bibb Latané (1968) set out to investigate how the knowledge that others are present in an emergency situation may affect the degree to which each witness helps the victim. In order to do this, they created a simulated emergency situation in a psychological laboratory at New York University. In their study, students were brought into the lab and were told that they would be talking with a group of other students about college life. Each of the students was seated in separate rooms, and was told that the discussion would be held via microphone in order to ensure the anonymity of the discussants. In fact, there was only one student who participated at a time, and the other "voices" were tape recordings designed to give the illusion that there were other people present in the study.

Because Darley and Latane were interested in investigating how the presence of other people influenced helping behavior, they varied the number of others who were supposedly "present" in the other room. Some of the participants in their study were told that there was only one other student present, others were told that there were two others present, and a third group were told that there were five others present. In order to create a simulated emergency situation, shortly after the discussion began, a tape recording of one of the other "students" came on indicating that he was having an epileptic seizure. On the recording, the student asked for help and then the tape became silent.

Results from this study were dramatic. The number of people that participants thought were in the study greatly impacted whether each student individually took steps to provide assistance. More than 80% of the students who believed that they were alone with the student having the "seizure" immediately rose to help the other person. In contrast, only about 60% of those who believed that one other person was available to help provided immediate assistance, and, shockingly, only about 30% of those who thought that five others were present provided aid. This study was important in showing that the mere presence of other people in a situation can have a large effect on how individuals in the situation will behave.

Other psychological research has shown that the mere presence of other people can also influence people's task performance. This phenomenon is known as social facilitation. Studies on social facilitation have shown that under certain conditions, people show increased performance on some tasks when they perform them in front of an audience. In the first study of this phenomenon, conducted more than a century ago, Triplett (1898) found that athletes, in this case bicycle riders, had faster racing times when they were racing as a group than when they were trying their best, but racing alone against a clock. Although the presence of an audience has been shown to increase performance on a wide variety of tasks such as typing, buying and selling in on-line auctions, and even performance at tug-of-war, other research has suggested that audiences do not always lead to increased performance.

Research since Triplett's study on bicycle racers has shown that the presence of other people increases performance only on tasks that performers are comfortable with—those that are easy, well-rehearsed, and well-practiced. In contrast, the presence of an audience actually decreases people's performance on tasks that are anxiety-producing—those that are complicated and poorly learned. To illustrate this distinction, Michaels, Blommel, Brocato, Linkous, and Rowe (1982) examined how good and poor pool players performed when they were unaware they were being observed and when they were in front of an audience. His study found that good pool players showed evidence of the social facilitation effect—their performance increased when they were in front of an audience as compared to how they performed when they were not aware that they were being observed. Poor pool players, on the other hand, not only did not show the social facilitation effect, but actually showed the opposite. Because they were not comfortable with their pool skills, the poor players performed worse when in front of an audience than when they were under the impression that they were alone.

THE SOCIAL CONTEXT OF COMPUTING

Just as we have seen that the social context can influence behavior and performance in emergency situations and in task performance, the social context in which children perform computer tasks can have a large impact on how successful students are when performing computer tasks in the classroom. However, because few educators are aware of the degree to which social context factors influence performance, oftentimes classrooms are set up in such a way that exacerbates the problem rather than minimizing it. Consider the following example. Ms. Kristina Martin is a teacher at Jackson Junior High. She has been thinking of the surprise that she has for her students when they arrive at class. Mrs. Martin has chosen an educational software program for her biology course that she believes is pedagogically excellent. This computer-based lesson will enable the children to see animated cartoon-like fish interact in a simulated aquatic environment. By manipulating the keys on their computers, they will be able to remove various elements of the fish's normal environment and learn of the consequences to the fish and marine life. The computer program is instructional and efficient. Its colorful display screen is a pleasure to behold.

Ms. Martin is probably correct in believing the computer-assisted software has the potential to motivate and teach children aspects of marine biology. What Mrs. Martin does not know is that the structure of the room in which the children sit will play a large role in determining how much they get out of the lesson. In her room, as in most classrooms, the children will sit at their desks or tables, working side by side as they prepare their lesson. Each student working at the computer is flanked by other students who are also working at computers and by students engaged in other activities. The presence of the other children will dramatically affect the performance of the children on their IT tasks.

Who Is Negatively Impacted by the Social Context?

If we reflect on the research on social facilitation, we know that the presence of others increases performance on well-learned tasks, and is detrimental to performance on poorly learned or anxiety-producing tasks. As we showed in our review of gender differences in computer anxiety in chapter 2, females experience a high level of anxiety when they work with computer programs that have been designed with the features that are attractive to boys. In that chapter, we outlined several possible reasons for these gender differences in reactions to computers. Because girls are less involved with video games as an extracurricular activity, they are not as used to or comfortable with the video game-like "bells and whistles" that characterize many of the computer-assisted instructional programs being used in today's classrooms. Additionally, most computer tasks are male-oriented even beyond their video game-like qualities—that is, they have many of the formal features that males prefer. Furthermore, societal stereotypes have imbued the field of computing with a reputation of being a generally male-oriented area. Females may also experience anxiety when attempting computer tasks because this reputation may lead them to have lower expectations for their own performance.

As a result of a combination of such factors, we know that many females experience anxiety when working with computers. The research on social facilitation suggests that this anxiety will interact with the presence of others in a classroom. As a consequence, when computing in public, we can predict that girls, on average, will end up performing less well on school tasks that take place on the computer or the Internet. Boys, on the other hand, will not experience the same level of computer anxiety, and thus, when engaging in computer tasks, will not typically mind the presence of others. In fact, similar to the way that expert pool players actually performed *better* when they were being watched by an audience, for boys who are comfortable with their computer skills, sometimes an audience may be the motivation they need to do a better job. The audience problem that affects girls and boys is of major importance and is multi-determined. Social facilitation is one of the social psychological factors that contribute to the gender difference. As we will detail in subsequent chapters, psychological processes including complex stereotyping and expectancy confirmation converge on the same conclusion: When the social context for technological learning includes groups of children, the performance of girls is likely to suffer.

And so, when Martha and Jared work on their classroom computers, Jared will prefer working in the presence of others. He will feel motivated, try more solutions, and have greater success. That very same context, however, will likely increase Martha's level of stress. She will feel more anxiety than Jared, probably feel more reticent to try novel solutions and, overall, will perform less well. Research has also shown that this difference is not due to an innate ability to learn from computers. In fact, Martha may do as well as Jared, and feel as calm as Jared, if she has her own computer and no one is able to watch over her shoulder. But the presence of her classmates will heighten the computer anxiety felt by Martha and most of the girls in her class, which will lead them to perform less well than the boys in the classroom.

Bucking the Trend: Gender and Social Groups

There is some irony to our suggestion that girls are uncomfortable computing in the presence of others. Typically, females are much more comfortable in groups than are males. Anyone who has had the opportunity to observe teenagers, for example, knows that teenage girls tend to have more expansive social groups than teenage boys, are more expressive and compassionate with their comrades, and prefer the company of others. Ample research has corroborated these observations (Anderson, 1999; Bank, 1995; Belle, 1989; Polimeni, Hardie, & Buzwell, 2002). It is also true that girls tend to do quite well in so-called "cooperative learning tasks" where the outcome of a lesson depends on the cooperation and communication among peers (Dalton, Hannafin, & Hooper, 1989; Johnson, Johnson, Richards, & Buckman, 1986). So, it is not that females shun social groupings or are less comfortable in the presence of others. To the contrary, computing in the presence of other people may make Martha more anxious *despite* her general proclivity to enjoy social groups. The irony of computer anxiety is that it is manifested in a public context if, and only if, the computing task is one that provokes anxiety in the first place. As we noted at the beginning of this chapter, social facilitation, or the fact that audiences increase performance on tasks on which people feel comfortable and decrease performance on tasks on which people feel anxious or uncomfortable, is a very basic psychological finding. Currently, for girls and women, it is typically the case that the presence of others will inhibit their performance.

Computing With a Classmate: Shedding Light on the Theory

The research we examine first was conducted in the United Kingdom with 11- and 12-year-old boys and girls (Light, Littleton, Bale, Joiner, & Messer, 2000). The children participated in a very cute IT task in which they needed to help a group of partying honey bears solve a logistical problem. In the "Honeybears" task, originally devised by Littleton, Light, Joiner, Messer, and Barnes (1992) and shown in the Fig. 3.1, the children's goal is to find a route by which the teddy bears, who were picnicking at Almwood, could recover the honey that they had left at Flint without its falling prey to the Honeymonsters. As the children progress in the task, they learn that Honeymonsters steal honey from any boat crossing the river, so a new way has to be found to get it across the river. The children have to find the proper solution, which is to transport the Honeybears to Flint via balloon. The children must discover the hidden information that leads to the balloon solution, while also learning about the system's constraints (e.g., how the bears move, how many can move, how the boats move, and so forth).

The Honeybears task is such that progress toward the ultimate goal can be measured numerically. The more information the children discovered, the higher their score. The closer they came to bringing the honey back to Almwood, the higher their score. Performance was measured on a scale ranging from zero (the children failed to make any move) to 6 (the children found the honey and brought it all the way back, without complication from the Honeymonsters.

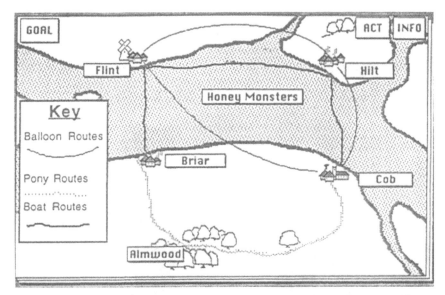

FIG. 3.1. The map presented to children in the "Honeybears" task used by Light et al. (2000) and by Littleton et al. (1992). The children's task is to recover the honey they left at Flint. From Light, P., Littleton, K., Bale, S., Joiner, R., & Messer, D. (2000). Gender and social comparison effects in computer-based problem solving. *Learning and Instruction, 10,* 483–496, Copyright © 2000, with permission from Elsevier.

Children played this adorable game in groups of two. Each child had a computer, each could see the other working, but each person worked at his or her own machine and each had his or her progress measured separately. In half of the cases, the two children were of the same sex. In the other half, the children were of the opposite sex. How well did they perform?

The results of Light et al.'s (2000) experiment showed clearly that the boys who worked in two-person dyads outperformed girls. As Fig. 3.3b shows, boys significantly outperformed girls on the Honeybears task. The second question that Light et al. asked is whether children would be more or less affected by being in single-sex or mixed-sex groups. Presumably, all children would experience greater anxiety in the presence of an 11- or 12-year-old of the opposite sex. This should lead to greater social facilitation. For girls, this should mean more anxiety, and less positive performance. For boys, this should mean greater challenge and motivation to get the right answer quickly on this computerized adventure game.

Figure 3.2 shows that this is precisely what happened. Boys showed improved performance in mixed-sex groups, whereas girls who computed in mixed-sex groups showed the poorest performance of all. The statistical interaction was significant. Whether Jared and Martha are learning reading in kindergarten, guiding Honeybears on their adventures in the sixth grade, or learning biology in the ninth grade, Martha will have a problem when working on IT software in public. In those rare cases in which their teachers find software that has the formal features girls adore and boys shun, then computing in public may cause boys to show performance decrements and girls to show better performance (Cooper, Hall, & Huff,

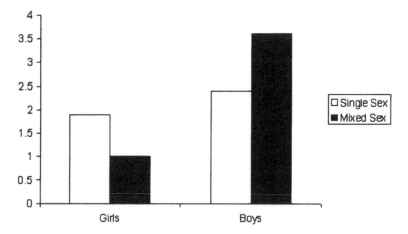

FIG. 3.2. Gender differences in performance depending on whether learning group is single sex or mixed sex (adapted from Light et al., 2000).

1990). But in the usual cases, where the IT software has the formal features that boys prefer, the boys will prosper when computing in the presence of others. The girls will not be so fortunate. They will experience computer anxiety and stress. They will also learn less from their teacher's well-intentioned computer lessons.

Computing in Public and Private: Re-Examining Demolition Division

In chapter 2, we presented research showing that girls experienced greater anxiety than boys when learning from Demolition Division, and that boys experienced greater anxiety than girls when learning with Arithmetic Classroom. We now re-examine those conclusions in light of the current discussion. Let's look more closely at that research. What was the social milieu in which the computing was conducted?

Indeed, the data presented in the previous chapter came from students who used computers in a public room. Recall that we found that, when students used the computer program that was male-oriented, girls experienced far more anxiety than did boys. Demolition Division's fast paced competitive action within a war game metaphor raised the anxiety level for the sixth-grade girls. Conversely, the verbal feedback emphasis of the Arithmetic Classroom program caused stress and anxiety for the boys. The results of this research came exclusively from children who performed the computer-assisted instruction task in a public context.

Let's visualize the look of the computer room that was introduced in the previous chapter. Each child sat in front of a computer screen. To his or her left and right were other children with the same assignment and provided with similar computers. Most were intent on their computer task; others milled about. The situation was probably fraught with less social anxiety than Light et al.'s (2000) study because the only children present were of the same gender. Girls were brought to the computer room without any boys present; similarly, boys only worked on their programs in the presence of other boys.

Hall, Huff, and I (Cooper et al., 1990) knew that if we wanted to examine how the social context impacted performance, it would be crucial to compare the results we obtained in this context with the anxiety and performance results of children who computed entirely alone. (A condition in which children worked entirely alone was not included in the study by Light et al., 2000.) For this reason, we had additional groups of students perform the computer tasks alone so we could use their results for comparison. In the "alone" conditions, the middle school children worked with the same computer-assisted instruction software that the children in the public conditions used. They were given the same instructions, tested for their ability at solving division problems and were given the Mattson Anxiety Scale. The only difference between children in this "alone" condition and the children described in the previous chapter (those in the "others present" condition) is that these children came to a computer in a school room without any other children present. Each boy or girl faced Demolition Division or Arithmetic Classroom on his or her computer without any child or adult present. Did it make a difference? The answer is a resounding yes.

In the following figure, we present the data from boys and girls who were by themselves when they studied the division problems using the programs Demolition Division or Arithmetic Classroom. As can be seen on the graph in Fig. 3.3, there are no meaningful differences between the anxiety levels expressed by boys and by girls when they used the program by themselves. As in the data we looked at before, Demolition Division is a more stressful exercise than Arithmetic Classroom. The quick pace of the competition, the demand for eye-hand coordination, and the exploding tanks or canons yielded higher stress scores for everyone. However, the differences between males and females that were so dramatic when the children worked in the presence of others is completely absent from the current data.

Taken together, the results take the form of a three-way statistical interaction. Anxiety is predicted by a combination of three variables: the gender of the learner, the formal features of the program, and the context in which the children did their computing. We saw the importance of two of these variables in the previous chapter. Males experience anxiety when working with a computer program that has the formal features preferred by females. Females experience anxiety when working with a program

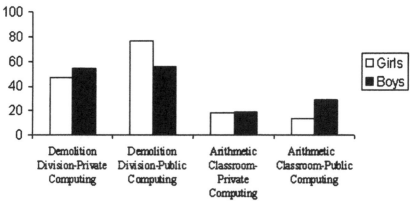

FIG. 3.3.   Anxiety level depending on social context and sex-typed nature of software (adapted from Cooper, Hall, & Huff, 1990).

containing the formal features preferred by males. To this we can now add the qualification: *when using the computer in the presence of others*.

WHAT IS STRESSFUL ABOUT OTHER PEOPLE?

What is it that bothers people about computing in public? As briefly mentioned before, there are many reasons that the presence of others might increase anxiety. Perhaps people worry about competition. If girls expect that they will not do well at a computer game, then they may be more worried than boys about the outcome of the competition. If Martha looks at the format of Demolition Division, she may anticipate that she will not do well at this boy-oriented game whose metaphor is war and destruction, and whose format requires so many of the activities that she would rather avoid. Martha may or may not consciously reason that boys will outperform girls on this task. In fact, when Light and his colleagues asked their U.K. children whether boys or girls are better at computer tasks, one third of the children of each gender said it was the boys. Not a single boy nor a single girl indicated that girls are better at computer tasks.

The Problem of Competition

Many school environments are notorious for their reliance on competition. The desire to out-perform one's peers is often used to motivate students to reach the peak of their performance. For older children, classroom grades, academic advancement, and admission to higher education all rely on one's academic standing relative to other children. As we have suggested, girls like Martha have been given an abundance of reasons to believe that they will not do as well as boys in IT competition. The mere fact that Martha knows that learning a lesson on a computer is not a task at which she is likely to do well is sufficient to be both demoralizing and anxiety arousing. We should not be surprised that these emotions alone will lead to poorer performance on an IT task.

The results of empirical studies confirm the deleterious effects of group competition on girls' performance on IT tasks. Imagine three broad types of structured computer lessons in the classroom. One may be called *individualistic* and calls for students to take turns performing the activity, with evaluation focused on the individual student's performance. A second may be *cooperative*, in that students perform tasks in groups, and the achievement of one group member is linked to that of his or her fellow group member. If one member of the group performs well, the other members benefit. A third structure is *competitive*. In this group structure, if one group member performs well in competitive learning situations, the other group members will fare more poorly by comparison.

The effect of individualistic, cooperative, and competitive learning environments was studied by Johnson, Johnson, and Stanne (1985). In their research, eighth-grade students learned geography using an interesting IT simulation. They learned to use the positions of the stars, the position of the sun, ocean depth, climate, and trade winds to navigate an ancient ship to a new continent in search of gold. Learning the daily geography lessons made it possible for the students to overcome obstacles (such as being stranded at sea or being attacked by pirates) that the computer program put in their paths. Thus, once again, an adventure metaphor subtly reminded the students that the task was one that communicated to boys more than to girls.

In their study, Johnson and his colleagues randomly placed students in an individualistic learning condition, a cooperative learning condition, or a competitive learning condition. Students in the cooperative condition were placed in four-person, gender-balanced groups and were given roles to play (e.g., captain, meteorologist) that helped them share their knowledge with each other. They were to be given individual daily quizzes and an individual final test to assess their knowledge, but they were told that their grade on the unit would be calculated by averaging the individual scores of each of the members of their group. Therefore, it was to each person's advantage that everyone else in the group learn their information and perform well on the exams.

In the competitive condition, students were also placed in gender-balanced groups of four children, but the rules were different. Students in the competitive condition were told that their final grades would be based on how they performed relative to the other members of their group and that they would receive bonus points for finishing before other students in the class. Students in the individual condition were simply told that they would complete the quizzes and the final alone and that they should do their own work.

The results of the quizzes and final exam showed that the structure of the computer learning environment made an important difference in students' learning. Students in the competitive condition learned significantly less geography and performed more poorly on the IT task than students in the individualistic or cooperative conditions. Students in the cooperative learning condition performed best.

The effect of group structure in Johnson et al.'s study was more important for girls than it was for boys. Girls performed just as well as boys in the individualistic and the cooperative learning conditions. Competitive instructions, however, had a particularly detrimental effect on the girls. They learned less geography and scored more poorly on the daily quizzes and final exams than did the boys. Although having to compete with peers in the technology lesson affected everyone, it hurt the girls the most.

In fact, the competitive environment had wide ranging and invidious effects that went beyond girls' reduced mastery of geography. In a follow-up survey, girls who had been in the competitive condition reported that they *liked* geography less than did the other children in the classroom, including the boys who had also been in the competitive condition. Moreover, the girls in the competitively structured groups felt that they had received less support from their learning environment, perceiving the teacher as insufficiently helpful. Girls in the competitive condition also reported liking computers less and reported that they were less confident in their ability to use computers than were their male counterparts. Recall that children were assigned to their learning condition *at random*. There were no systematic differences in knowledge or attitudes prior to their being placed in one of the three learning environments. This forces us to conclude that being in a competitive group environment for their geography lessons caused girls to learn less and also caused them to feel negatively about their own ability at computers, forming more negative attitudes toward information technology in the process.

Beyond Competition: Other Effects of the Social Context

Why else might a girl in Ms. Martin's class experience anxiety? Perhaps it is not only competition *per se*, but just the knowledge of how she compares to her classmates that is upsetting. If Martha's friend is also performing the biology exercise, looking at each other perform can provide knowledge of how each of them stacks up against the other, and this might be the cause of stress. This is not competition in the sense of their being some clear standard for who "wins" or whether there is a reward (e.g., an A or a prize) for good performance. Rather, it is the knowledge of where one stands relative to others that can be both informative and potentially upsetting. If Martha sees her friend working away at the task or if she believes that her friend is observing or overhearing Martha work on the task, then stress and anxiety may occur for both of them. In the male-oriented biology program, or in Demolition Division, neither Martha nor her friend will likely feel optimistic about their performances and each may expect the results of the social comparison to be stressful.

A still simpler version of why public contexts are stressful is the mere knowledge that someone else will know how you did at a task. Especially when the task is one at which you do not expect to do well, then the mere knowledge that someone else knows how you are doing may cause anxiety. In this version of a public context, it is not necessary for a person to be competing with another for a reward, nor need there be any question of who is better or worse at a particular task. In this version, some other person's knowledge of how well you performed may be sufficient to arouse anxiety. We investigate this question in the next section.

MEN AND WOMEN PLAY "ZORK": A CLOSER LOOK AT WHAT CONSTITUTES PUBLIC

Kris Robinson-Stavely and I took another look at the social context of computing to examine these questions (Robinson-Stavely & Cooper, 1990). We also wanted to expand the study of gender-based computer anxiety to adults as well as children. To do this, we invited Princeton University students to participate in a study in which they would play a computer game in the research laboratory. The game we chose for them was an adventure game, Zork. Zork is a clever computer program in which the player attempts to locate the existence of a treasure. The metaphor for the program is male-oriented: Finding the treasure requires participating in an adventure in which dragons must be slain, evil characters fought and vanquished, and physical obstacles overcome. The player may interact with the computer by telling the protagonist how to move through the adventure environment. The computer responds with written words to tell the player if he or she has made progress toward the goal, or whether he or she has been met by an obstacle or evil opponent who is trying to protect the treasure.

Zork was an ideal computer task for research purposes. In a manner similar to Honeybears, the game has a specific goal, and people's progress toward the goal can be measured. Therefore, we could not only find out if playing the computer game created anxiety under specific, predictable circumstances, but we could also measure the degree of success people had.

Our students volunteered to play Zork as a part of a research study. We told them about the game, and then brought them to the room in which the computer was located. They needed only a few words of instructions to begin the game. Because the adventure format of Zork made it the kind of game that has the formal features the males like, we predicted that the women in our study would experience anxiety and that their performance would not be as successful as males.

But what of the social context? Does it matter whether the students engaged in the Zork task alone or in the presence of others? The results of our study with middle school children already demonstrated that anxiety is manifested only in the social or public context. Would the same phenomenon happen with older students? Our prediction was that it would—that computer anxiety would occur primarily, or perhaps only, in the presence of other people.

This prediction still leaves us in a quandary about what we mean by the term "other people around." Specifically, we were interested in looking at what it is about the public nature of the computing context that causes the expression of anxiety at a cross-gender task. We have discussed three possibilities that may make a public context conducive to experience anxiety. First, there was competition—expecting that you will lose to other people who are also performing the task. Second, there was social comparison—the knowledge that you and others may acquire about where you stack up among people in your group. Third, there was mere knowledge—the cognition that some other person or persons will know how you performed. Each of these may create anxiety if the nature of the computer task is one that communicates that it is a task at which you are not expected to do very well.

Robinson-Stavely and I decided to test a fourth and simplest meaning of the concept of a public context—the mere co-existence of other people in one's social environment. For the other three possible representations of public context in the mind of an individual, there had to be some reasonable complexity in the structure of the social context. People needed to be performing the same task. They had to have knowledge of each other's performance and needed some way to interpret the meaning either of the final product of the computing or a way to interpret the meaning of what was on each other's computer screen. All of these complexities are reasonable in most computing situations. They were likely to have been present when Martha, Jared and their classmates set out to work on Ms. Martins' biology program. All of these possibilities existed when British sixth-grade children in the study by Light et al. (2000) and American sixth-grade children in the study by Cooper et al. (1990) computed in the public condition at their middle schools.

In this study, we wanted to begin with the simplest of all meanings of "public" context—what we might call "mere presence." Our hypothesis is that in a male-oriented adventure game, women will experience computer anxiety just because someone else is present in a room. If we eliminate competition, if we eliminate knowledge of the other's performance, and any other complicating factor, the mere presence of another person will still foment anxiety in the computer user.

When a university student agreed to play Zork in our study, we ushered him or her to the room in which the computer was set up to play the game. For half of the participants, there was no one else in the room and he or she proceeded to begin the game. For the other half of the participants, another person was already seated at the far end of the room, working on a computer. The researcher indicated to the participant that the computer that was vacant was the computer on which Zork was loaded. The researcher also apologized that the research team could not locate a room in which there was only a single computer.

"I apologize," said the experimenter, "but we only have computer 'clusters' in this building. There is obviously someone else here who is working on something, but, whatever it is, it has nothing whatsoever to do with what you have to do."

Then, making contact with the other person (who, unbeknownst to the subject was actually a confederate hired for the experiment), the researcher said she hoped we would not be disturbing her. "That's all right," remarked the other person, "I'm only writing a letter." With this information we made clear to the research participant that (a) another student was present at the computer but (b) that student could neither compete nor have any awareness of the participant's performance since she was doing something entirely different on her computer.

We also thought it advisable to have the confederate the same gender as the research participant. Although it is surely interesting in its own right, we did not want to complicate the effects of the presence of other people with social concerns in a mixed-gender situation. In the public condition, therefore, the letter-writing confederate was male if the participant was male, female if the participant was female.

After each participant played Zork for 30 minutes, we asked him or her to stop. Following the game, each participant was given a battery of questionnaires including an adult version of the Mattson anxiety questionnaire that we used in the research presented in the previous chapter. The computer automatically tracked each player's progress toward the goal, which gave us a measure of performance to complement the anxiety measure.

Zork is a male-oriented computer game. Did females experience anxiety? The results of the Mattson anxiety measure show that they did—but *only* if they computed in the presence of another person. Look at the anxiety that our participants reported in Fig. 3.4. It shows that, when another person was present, women reported considerably more anxiety than men (mean scores of 4.6 for females vs. 3.3 for males). However, when

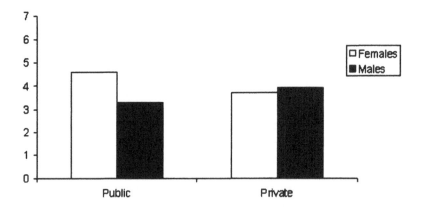

FIG. 3.4.   Gender differences in reported anxiety while working with Zork in public versus in private. Adapted from Robinson-Stavely & Cooper, 1990, Mere presence, gender, and reactions to computers: Studying human-computer interaction in the social context. *Journal of Experimental Social Psychology, 26,* 168–183, copyright © 1990, with permission from Elsevier.

they computed in private, there was no meaningful difference in reported anxiety (means of 3.7 and 3.9 for women and men, respectively).

Now let's look at performance scores. How well did male and female college students do at solving the computer task presented by Zork? Once again, the social context was critical. When working alone, female students outperformed male students by a wide margin. The score for male students averaged 6.7. The average score for females was 19.1. However, when another person was present, the data completely turned around. This time, males' performance scores soared to 16.3, while the score for females plummeted to 1.4.

These data teach us that women can perform as well as men on the computer task. In fact, for this particular task, they can perform a great deal better—provided that they compute in a private context. Perhaps our female participants were more adept at this task; perhaps they were more motivated than the male students for this particular task. Either way, they showed their ability to succeed at Zork as long as they were alone. However, in the presence of another student—even though that other student was the same gender as the participant and was doing something completely different from the Zork game and paying no apparent attention to the Zork player—the female participants experienced great anxiety, and their performance collapsed. By contrast, males seemed to rise to whatever challenge the presence of another person created. With the confederate present, males kept their anxiety in check and achieved significantly higher scores.

The data also offer a glimpse at how the differences in anxiety turned into differences in performance scores. We know that, in the presence of other people, female college students were more anxious and achieved

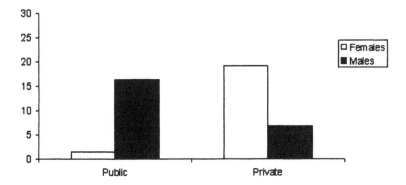

FIG. 3.5.   Gender differences in computer performance while working with Zork in public versus in private. Adapted from Robinson-Stavely & Cooper, 1990, Mere presence, gender, and reactions to computers: Studying human-computer interaction in the social context. *Journal of Experimental Social Psychology, 26,* 168–183, copyright © 1990, with permission from Elsevier.

lower scores on the computer task. The computer was able to record another statistic that we have labeled "Actions." An action is an attempt to do something in response to a dilemma posed by the Zork adventure. For example, if the computer wrote to a player indicating that there was a monster located to the east and north of the player, one action might be to turn the protagonist's character to the south. This may turn out to be a productive action on the player's part, allowing him or her to avoid a confrontation and make progress toward the goal. Alternatively, the player may choose to turn north. This would not be a productive action because it would result in an altercation that would, at the very least, allow valuable minutes to go by without making progress toward finding the treasure. A second alternative might be for a player to sit at his or her computer, unsure of which action to take and, consequently, do nothing. The first two courses are considered "actions" because the player took measures to solve the dilemma. Even though only one of the choices was correct, both would be scored similarly as actions. Only the second alternative, doing nothing, would be scored differently because no action was taken.

How did our research participants do? The data presented in Fig. 3.6 show clear and significant differences on the "action" measure. When alone, both males and females took a moderate number of actions in response to their dilemmas (6.7 and 7.0, respectively). The difference between these numbers is trivial and not statistically significant. On the other hand, males working with Zork in the presence of others not only had their anxiety reduced (as we saw in the figures presented earlier), but also raised the number of actions to a mean of 13.0. Females working in the presence of others had their anxiety level raised and, as the figure shows, they took very few actions. Their mean number of actions fell to 4.1. Thus,

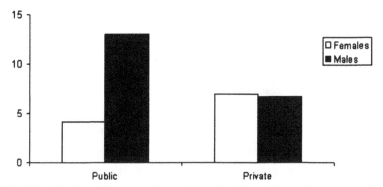

FIG. 3.6. Gender differences in number of actions taken when computing in public and in private. Adapted from Robinson-Stavely & Cooper, 1990, Mere presence, gender, and reactions to computers: Studying human-computer interaction in the social context. *Journal of Experimental Social Psychology, 26,* 168–183, copyright © 1990, with permission from Elsevier.

in the presence of other people, the picture for female players in this male-oriented action game was to experience significantly greater stress than males or than females who worked on the game alone. Their response was to lower their output—that is, to stop trying. They took very few right or wrong actions and, as a result, their scores plummeted. Males, whose performance was mediocre at best when playing alone, lowered their anxiety in public performances. They responded by trying lots of things, some of them right and some of them wrong. But the act of trying allowed them to find enough correct solutions to their dilemmas to raise their final performance scores.

In Allentown, Pennsylvania, Judy Lichtman (1998) observed the way middle-school girls and boys behaved on computers. Her observations correspond to our findings. She observed, "When girls do sit down at a computer, they tend to wait for instructions and blame themselves when something doesn't work. In contrast, boys often approach technology with an aggressive, experimental attitude, clicking their way to a solution … Boys develop confidence which comes from an intimate knowledge and mastery of technology" (p. 2).

Thus, research shows that the social context makes a huge difference in how well people use the computer and how comfortable they are while doing it. Public performances seem to result in anxiety for people using computer programs that are primarily designed for the other gender. Yet, these effects occurred even when the public nature of the performance was minimal indeed. In our study, there was no communication between the computer user and the person sharing his or her room. There was no opportunity for competition or social comparison, nor was there any chance the stranger in the room could have knowledge of the student's performance. It almost seems that the mere presence of another person magically transformed men into high computer achievers and women into highly anxious users with limited achievement. We would imagine that, as in the laboratory of Light et al. (2000), these effects would only be exacerbated in situations in which the girls and boys actually felt like their peers or others were watching them, measuring them, and gauging how well they did on the computer task.

Anxiety is both a cause and an effect of boys' and girls' different levels of performance at the computer. Because anxiety interferes with complex learning, it drives down girls' level of accomplishment. With repeated exposures, the mere thought of having to work at a computer creates a further expectation of relative failure, which, in turn, increases the level of anxiety and stress. The cycle almost certainly continues, and grows more automatic with repeated occurrences. In the Robinson-Stavely and Cooper (1990) research, we conducted a second experiment that was designed to provide one way to break the cycle.

For reasons we have already discussed (and because of other factors we discuss in subsequent chapters), girls expect that they will not do well at computational tasks, especially when they perform those tasks in the presence of others. Boys expect otherwise. Relative to girls, they have confidence in their ability to take on computational tasks and are even more determined to show it in the presence of others. Boys' expectations arouse confidence that leads to heightened performance. Girls' expectations beget anxiety, which, in turn, produces poorer performance at the computer. In our second study, we wondered what would happen if we changed girls' expectations and cause them to anticipate that they would be superb at using the computer. For practical reasons, we thought that it was too tall an order to change anyone's estimation of their overall ability in a field of endeavor in one experimental session. (The current authors know, for example, that if we were told that we should expect to play chess like chess masters, it would be a very tough sell indeed!) On the other hand, it might be possible to convince someone that she will do very well at a particular computer task, regardless of how well or poorly she may have done with information technology in the past.

Robinson-Stavely and Cooper's second study again featured Princeton University students playing the game of Zork. As in the first experiment (reported earlier), half of the males and half of the females played Zork alone; the other half played with the mere coexistence of someone else in the room. In the second experiment, however, we systematically manipulated males and females expectations of how successful they will be at Zork. Before starting the game, each student was seated alone at a computer and filled out what appeared to be a psychological survey assessing their personal characteristics and prior experiences. When they were finished, the computer automatically "scored" their questionnaire and provided them with feedback about how they could expect to do at the Zork task. Unbeknownst to the participants, the feedback was actually written by the experimenters and came in one of two versions. In the "Expect Success" condition, the feedback stated, "The test results from your interest and personality inventory tell us that you will do very well at the game of Zork. Your profile matches the types of skills required by the task. Regardless of how you have done in the past at computer tasks, you should expect to do very well at this game."

Students in the "Expect Failure" condition were provided with less optimistic news. They were told, "The test results from your interest and personality inventory tell us that you will probably not do very well at the game of Zork. Your profile shows skills and interests that may interfere with successful performance. Regardless of how you have done in the past at computer tasks, you should not expect to do very well at this game."

Following the feedback, students were given a description of the Zork game. After reading about the game, they were given a short survey that included a crucial question about how they expected to do at the game of Zork. Most participants responded to the crucial question in a way that indicated they believed the manipulation. Regardless of their overall skill level at computers, they came to expect that, *on this particular task,* they would do well or poorly, depending on the feedback that they had received from their personality and interest test. Of course, not everyone believed the manipulation, and it is informative to look at who did and who did not believe the feedback. When students were told that they probably would not do well, 19 out of 20 women believed the manipulation. Men believed it, too, with 17 out of 20 indicating that they did not expect to do well. What is particularly interesting is the result in the positive expectancy condition. Men tended to believe the manipulation, with 74% (14 out of 19) expecting to succeed. When women were told to expect success at Zork, the percentage who believed the manipulation dropped to 55%. Nine of the 20 women thought that they would not be able to do well at Zork.

Nonetheless, when we examined the performance of our university students at the Zork game, we saw evidence of the pattern we had predicted. Considering only the students who believed our manipulation, we found that students who were led to believe they would be successful were more successful than students who expected to fail. As we predicted, this was mostly true when the computing was done in the presence of others. Furthermore, it was equally true of both sexes. Men *and* women who expected to fail showed a pattern of results just like the pattern that women showed in the first experiment. Men *and* women who expected to succeed showed a pattern just like the men's pattern in the first experiment. In other words, when women's previously learned tendency to think they would not do well was overridden by our specific instruction that they could expect to excel at this particular task, then they performed quite well. And, consistent with our analysis of the stress-arousing nature of the presence of others, these results occurred only in the public context.

The results are depicted in Fig. 3.7. When expecting success in the public context, students achieved a score of 17.4, the highest of all of the scores. When expecting failure in a public context, they scored only 11.3, the lowest achievement of all of the conditions. Computing in private produced scores in the mid-range (15.0 and 12.1) that were not statistically different from one another. When students were asked about their level of stress, they showed the predicted response. For men and women, the level of stress and general anxiety was highest when computing in the presence of other people while under the burden of expecting to fail.

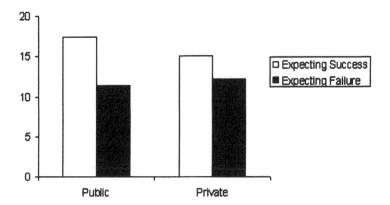

FIG. 3.7.   Differences in performance as a function of performance expectancy and social context. Adapted from Robinson-Stavely & Cooper, 1990, Mere presence, gender, and reactions to computers: Studying human-computer interaction in the social context. *Journal of Experimental Social Psychology, 26,* 168–183, copyright © 1990, with permission from Elsevier.

Our conclusion from this series of studies sounds both a pessimistic and an optimistic note. The pessimistic note is that people who feel they will not perform well at a computer task are under a special burden. Although they can cope with their expectation of failure while performing alone, they cannot overcome their burden in the presence of others. Anxiety and stress overwhelm them and interfere with their success. Performance tumbles, which probably undermines future expectations and enhances future levels of stress. The first study in the Robinson-Stavely and Cooper (1990) series shows that stress and computer anxiety resides most heavily in women and it is they who suffer in the presence of others. By contrast, the second study sounds the optimistic note. When given a believable expectation that they will succeed at an IT task, women perform just as well as men. They do not report anxiety and they are not troubled by the social context. We should be able to build upon this result to help level the computer playing field for men and women. We address this issue in chapter 6.

Beyond Stress: Social Context Affects Social Cognition

The social context of computing affects what people think as well as what they feel. To this point, we have highlighted the impact of the social context on children's motivations and emotions. Anxiety and stress dominate the performance of girls when they use IT programs in public, whereas boys seem to become more enthused, eager, and productive while computing in the public arena. There are also changes in what boys and girls think and remember when they compute in a public context, especially in mixed- sex groups.

Recall that, in a number of surveys, boys reported that they were more experienced with computers than were girls. Girls reported having negative attitudes toward computers and a higher degree of stress. Let's focus, though, on the survey results that show that girls report having less experience on the computer and having fewer computers in their homes than do the boys. There are two possibilities to ponder. One is the obvious explanation, and it is likely to be true. Families are less likely to purchase computers for their daughters than for their sons, and girls are less likely to use their computers than are boys. We do not doubt that these recollections are based on reality, but does it completely account for the finding? There is a second possibility that may amplify the differences between girls' and boys' memories of the availability and use of computers. It is possible that the social context exaggerates, and perhaps sometimes actually causes, the differences in the way boys and girls think about and remember their experiences with information technology. Girls and boys may retrospectively distort their level of computer experience in gender stereotypic ways.

Jeff Stone and I asked a group of middle school students a series of written questions about their computer use (Cooper & Stone, 1996). Specifically, they were asked how much time they typically spend using the computer each day—both at home and in school. All of the students answered our questions while seated with a small group of other children. In some of the groups, the gender composition was mixed. The other groups were either all boys or all girls. When girls filled out the survey in mixed-sex groups, they reported that they spent *less time* each day on the computer than did the girls who filled out the survey in a group with other girls. Precisely the opposite pattern was found for boys. When boys filled out the questionnaire in a mixed-sex group, they reported spending *more time* on the computer than when they responded in groups made up only of boys. In mixed company, boys and girls conformed to the stereotype of what is expected of people of their sex.

We would not be surprised by these results if the students answered in public. Boys may be motivated to strut their computer-literate feathers in front of the girls in their group, while girls may want to make a public show of shunning this boy-friendly technology. However, the middle school students in the Cooper and Stone study were reporting their computer-related judgments on a confidential questionnaire. Why did the girls report spending less time with IT when boys were present? Why did boys recall spending more time with computers when girls were present? We can only speculate about the process, but we believe the social context may produce cognitive distortions—that is, errors in the way people perceive and recall events in their environment.

It is likely that the presence of youngsters of the opposite sex causes boys and girls to think of themselves in terms of their gender. In chapter 5, we examine examples of this phenomenon when a solo member of one sex finds himself or herself in a group comprised exclusively of members of the other sex. Research on this phenomenon, often referred to as *tokenism*, shows the deleterious impact on people's cognitive abilities when they are solo representatives of their gender group. However, even when boys and girls are not solo members of their groups, the mere presence of the other group highlights their membership in a gender group. Thus, boys think of themselves more as boys, girls think of themselves more as girls, when the groups are of mixed gender.

When a girl thinks of herself as a girl, she is "primed" to think of behaviors and thoughts that are consistent with what she thinks is stereotypical of girls. It is not that she wants to lie about her computer use. Rather, when primed with the category of her gender, she is more likely to scan her memory for recollections consistent with her identity as a girl. Similarly, boys scan their memories for cognitions consistent with what boys stereotypically do and think. The boy, when his gender is highlighted, may recall his participation in sports, his interest in science, or his last trip to the video arcade. When asked about computer use, he vividly recalls the hours or minutes that he spent in front of the computer, playing games, doing homework, or surfing the Web. When the girl has her gender highlighted, she is more likely to remember her conversations with her friends and less likely to remember the time spent at the computer screen. In this way, just being in a group of boys and girls makes each person recall thoughts that are consistent with his or her gender stereotype. The boy exaggerates his recollection of his computer use and, by extension, his interest in information technology. The girl underrepresents her activity at the computer and, by extension, infers she has less interest in IT.

SEX COMPOSITION OF COMPUTER CLASSES

Not only does the social context of computing influence students' retrospective memories for the amount of time they spend on the computer, it also reminds them of society's expectations for their gender. A common theme that arose in many of our interviews with Princeton University freshmen was that there are pronounced gender differences in the number of boys and girls taking computer classes, advanced mathematics classes, and advanced physics classes in the high schools they attended. Our female students thought that the unequal gender distribution was detrimental in a variety of ways.

Karen, a student who had attended a public high school in Southern California, remembered, "There were about six girls in my AP Physics class as compared to about 34 guys. When I looked around at the students in the class, the societal belief that guys are better at this than girls came to my mind. I tried to tell myself that it was no big deal, that I can do this too." Karen continued, "We know that stereotypes are out there and we know that other students might feel a certain way. Maybe this unconsciously affects us."

Monica, a student who attended a public high school in Chicago, had a similar story: "I was the only girl in my physics class with eight boys. The first couple of weeks I felt very intimidated."

Women are also affected by the stories their friends tell them. Susan's best friend was the only female in an advanced math class in high school: "My friend used to tell me that she felt like she did not fit in. She would sit in the corner of the classroom and not talk to anyone. I wasn't very interested in taking that class."

Not only did our female students notice the gender disparity in many upper level math and science courses, some of the male students noticed it too. Elliot, a student from Atlanta offered, "The makeup of my math classes and computer classes was 70–80% male on average. Most of the girls, even if they were capable of the work, were turned off by the lack of females in the course."

Gender divides in course composition can influence students' perceptions in many different ways. Courses with unequal numbers of girls and boys may make stereotypes salient, and may send a message to girls and young women that the topic of study is not for them or people like them. Karen, for instance, had to remind herself several times that she too could do the work in physics. Teachers in these courses, who are overwhelmingly male, also may take a demonstrative male majority as an opportunity to gear the examples toward the male audience. Using examples such as sports statistics in math and computer classes can be alienating for the girls present, especially if they do not understand the relationships between the teams, the meaning of sports terminology, and so on. Like Denise from the previous chapter, one of our female students remembered this happening in her computer class in high school: "One teacher used a lot of sports examples, specifically the Celtics. But that's because he was a sports *fanatic*. You should've seen the guy's office! But I like sports so that wasn't a problem for me. But I can see how other girls might have felt unincluded in some class conversations because of it." Although this young woman was not bothered by the sports examples herself, one can easily see how it may turn off other girls and even make a course more difficult for girls. For instance, if batting average is used as a computer example, not knowing what it is makes the example more confusing and difficult to understand, above and beyond an already intimidating computer programming assignment.

In addition to making societal stereotypes salient, when the classroom social context skewed in favor of more boys, this can also inadvertently help confirm gender stereotypes. That is, when there are more boys than girls in a class, often the best student in the class is a boy. Students may see this as confirmation of the societal stereotypes, that boys are better at computers or math than girls. However, given the different base rates of boys and girls in the classes, it is more likely a consequence of the numbers. For instance, Karen noted that boys seemed to do better than girls in her physics class that had about 85% boys and 15% girls. When asked to explain *why* she thought the boys were better than the girls, she talked about research showing that boys have superior spatial relationships skills than girls. However, a more subtle and perhaps accurate reason might have simply been because there were 34 boys and 6 girls in the class, thus making it more probable that the top student would be a boy.

Interactions Between Boys and Girls in Unequal Classrooms

The students' stories also made it clear that gender disparities in courses can also lead to detrimental social dynamics between the majority group of boys and the minority group of girls. Nicole, a student from Virginia, for instance, was the only girl on her school's "Academic Team," a selective team that competed with other high schools on academic exercises. Nicole remembered that being the only girl was difficult and intimidating at times, and recalled that "the boys on the team used to make jokes about boys being smarter. I always pretended to laugh along with them at the jokes, but inside it really bothered me and even sometimes made me angry. I was the focus of attention and it was awkward. I wondered why they kept saying it when it really was not that funny at all."

In addition to facing what are essentially sexist jokes, some of our male students pointed out other social dynamics they saw in the classrooms. In particular, the male students remembered that young women in their courses often looked up to the young men for help on assignments and class projects. Lyle, a student from Connecticut who planned to major in molecular biology at Princeton, noted that, "In my higher math classes, the other males, but especially the females, looked to guys to know and solve every problem known to man."

Other young men noted similar dynamics in their courses. Steven, for instance, pointed out, "males were treated better [in advanced math and science courses] because the course seemed very male oriented. It is a common stereotype that engineers are males, and that the engineering field is geared toward males. Most of the males stuck it out just because they were males and they were expected to be better."

Others mirrored these comments. Greg mentioned, for instance, "Girls always assumed guys knew more so they would ask them for help."

Interestingly, at least one young woman had a difference recollection about whether girls were more likely to ask boys for help on assignments. Maria, for instance, remembered, "I noticed that several of the males in the class seemed to think it was their responsibility to help me if I was ever stuck or confused about something while we were in the computer lab writing programs. I preferred going to the teacher for help, though."

CONCLUSION: THE SOCIAL CONTEXT MATTERS

In conclusion, we see that the social context plays a very crucial role in encouraging or discouraging children's and adults' success with the computer. Our search of the literature finds very few differences in males' and females' competence with the computer, when they are using information technology by themselves. As soon as computing becomes public, however, the arrangement of the social context can make an enormous difference in the way people feel and think. Computer anxiety becomes exacerbated in public. Girls and boys become more motivated to conform to their social stereotypes, to the detriment of the girls' performance on the computer. Overall, males expect to succeed; girls worry about failing. Girls think of themselves as less computer literate and recall far fewer successful experiences on the computer than do boys.

As we have seen, the gender composition of children's groups when learning or performing an IT task plays a very important role in how children feel and think about themselves. However, the mere presence of others—even of the same gender—produces deleterious effects on girls' achievement. Nor do adults escape the invidious role played by the social group. Women continue to perform more poorly when computing in a social context.

It is not likely that public or private schools will be able to provide individual instruction in computing technology any time soon. One reason is that there are some very sound pedagogical advantages for group instruction across the school curriculum (E. Aronson, Stephan, Sikes, Blaney, & Snapp, 1978; Schlechter, 1990; Stephenson, 1994). Another reason is financial. Spending on IT in schools in the United States reached $6.5 billion in 1998–1999, achieving a computer-to-student ratio of 1 to 16. The cost to taxpayers of achieving a 1-to-1 ratio will be staggering. The question we will need to deal with, as educators and as members of society, is how to change the social context into a powerful instrument to create, rather than to undermine, equal opportunity and equal achievement. In chapter 6, we offer some suggestions to achieve this goal.

CHAPTER

4

Expectancies and the Computer

Expectancies often produce behaviors that confirm those expectancies. When we expect people to act, think, and feel in certain ways, we often unwittingly produce the actions, thoughts, and feelings we expected to see. In this chapter, we show that people's expectation about the differences between boys' and girls' interest and ability with computers is a crucially significant factor that actually produces those differences. They also play a major role in determining the types of educational computer software that, as we have already documented, play a major role in causing computer anxiety among females.

Let's once again consider our two kindergartners, Jared and Martha. As they head off to school, they may have no idea that people in society expect Martha to be better behaved than Jared, to listen to her teacher more attentively, and to be able to follow school rules more completely. They may have no idea that people expect Jared to be more interested in sports and competitive activities. And they may have no idea that people expect Jared, eventually, to be more interested and competent in science, mathematics, and computers. Parents, relatives, teachers, and other adults in society harbor these expectations, and the impact on boys and girls may be cumulative and severe.

In this chapter, we discuss psychological research showing that the expectancies that others have can affect our self-conceptions, our perceptions of others, and our behavior. Expectancies become self-fulfilling prophecies. Because someone has an expectation of how I should behave, that person may act unwittingly to bring about just the behavior he or she was expecting to see. If a person thinks I am loquacious, he or she may

67

act toward me in a way that actually encourages me to talk more. If that person thinks I am hostile, he or she may act in a way that causes me to be aggressive. And if a parent or teacher thinks that Martha is reluctant to use computers, then the adult may act in a way that will cause Martha to feel reluctance when facing the computer.

SOURCES OF EXPECTANCIES: TRUE AND NOT SO TRUE

Interpersonal expectancies emanate from many sources: Some are based on facts we know about a person, some are based on what others have told us about a person, others are based on stereotypes and group memberships. Expectancies can be accurate or inaccurate. Nonetheless, they affect the way the recipient of the expectancies acts and feels. We suggest that a combination of individual expectancies and group stereotypes operate in the home and the classroom to produce a self-fulfilling prophecy that leads girls such as Martha to experience computer anxiety and to question their ability to be competent users of today's technology.

Expectancies run rampant in any social situation where people interact. Schools are an early instance. Children have expectancies about their teachers. As we all can recall from own school careers, teachers came with "reputations." They were gentle, kind, or mean. As children, our expectations probably influenced our teacher's behavior to some extent. Teachers, too, had expectations about us. And they have expectations about the Jareds, Marthas, and most of the other children in their classes. Often the expectations are based on real events and are substantially accurate. For example, a teacher may expect that a child whose beautiful poem was published in the fourth-grade bulletin will continue to write well in the fifth grade. The third grader who won the spelling bee may be expected to rank high on his or her spelling assignments throughout the year. These expectations may not be completely accurate, but they are based on more than a mere kernel of truth.

Sometimes, the expectancies that teachers have for their students are based less on an individual's behavior and more on reputational factors. A teacher may expect a new student to do well because the student's brother or cousin did well a few years before. Or, of course, a student may be expected to be the class clown, because that was how his or her sibling behaved years ago.

Another source of expectancies is the group membership to which a student belongs. A teacher may adopt society's views about the stereotypic behavior of boys and girls; about children from wealthy and poor families; about children of different races. Or, the teacher may have his or her own views about what to expect from members of particular groups. We call these expectancies *stereotypes* because they are beliefs applied to each member of a group solely because of group membership, regardless of whether they are accurate for a particular individual. In some cases, stereotypes may be generally accurate and other cases woefully inaccurate. But even if they are accurate in a general sense, they do not necessarily apply to the individual with whom a person is interacting. Have you ever spoken to someone who was elderly and found yourself talking at an exaggerated volume? Without having to think about it very much, you speak louder in order to be understood. For many people, the mere presence of an elderly person makes us raise our voices, even if we have no specific reason to believe this particular elderly person has difficulty hearing. However, our stereotypes lead us to associate hearing difficulty with old age, and may lead us to expect that we are talking to someone who does not hear well. Only after the older person asks us to stop shouting do we realize that we have unconsciously modified our behavior in a stereotypic fashion. We may even be momentarily embarrassed for having had that particular expectation and somewhat surprised that we behaved accordingly. It is true that hearing in the elderly declines with age, but that generalization may be dreadfully wrong when applied to a particular person just because he or she is old.

THE SELF-FULFILLING PROPHECY IN THE CLASSROOM: FROM EXPECTANCY TO BEHAVIOR

The first research that showed dramatic effects of the self-fulfilling prophecy was conducted in elementary schools, and that would make a good place for us to begin our story. The classic study was conducted in California by Robert Rosenthal and Lenore Jacobson (1968). Their research question was whether teachers' expectations about the likely academic success of their students would lead to academic performance consistent with those expectations. If a teacher expected a student to perform well, would that expectation lead to greater academic success by the student? To study this, Rosenthal and Jacobson told elementary school teachers that some of the children in their classes had scored very high on a reliable academic test, the "Harvard Test of Inflected Acquisition." The designated students were expected to show remarkable improvement in academic performance during the year. However, the expectations were not really based on the Harvard Test. In fact, because the researchers were really interested in how the teachers' expectations affected children's performance, the researchers randomly selected some of the children in the classroom to be designated as high performers, and the rest to be labeled as average performers. The children's actual ability was not related to the expectations that the researchers gave to the teachers.

Results from Rosenthal and Jacobson's (1968) study showed that the children who had been designated as "high performers" ended up performing better on an IQ test given at the end of the school year than the children who had been labeled as average. Because the "high performer" designation was random and not in reality based on any test score, we can say with confidence that the students' increased performance was caused by the (false!) expectations that the researchers had communicated to the teachers. Apparently, simply expecting certain students to perform well (even if this expectation is based on misleading information transmitted by a third party) can lead them to do so.

Two Students Tell Their Stories

In Rosenthal and Jacobson's research, teachers' expectations were manipulated only in a positive direction. In the real world, expectations may take on negative characteristics. This is especially true of expectations based on gender and ethnicity. We interviewed incoming Princeton University students about their high school experiences as they were considering applying to college. Karen and Dominique related incidents about how even well-meaning college counselors' and teachers' unconscious gender expectancies almost hindered them from fulfilling their academic potential.

Karen is Hispanic, and her mother, who works as a housekeeper, does not speak English. Karen was an excellent student in her high school. She had taken one advanced placement class her sophomore year, and three AP classes during her junior year, and had received A's in all of them. Karen told her high school counselor that she wanted to take a full load of six AP courses her senior year. When the counselor questioned whether she would be able to handle the course load, Karen began to doubt her own ability, "When I went in to sign up for the senior year AP courses (the counselor) asked me are you *sure* you want to take all those courses? Isn't that too much? I was a bit confused about why she asked that. I knew that other people had done it before and I was thinking to myself why does she think that I can't do it too?"

When Karen went back to her guidance counselor to talk about college applications the counselor began their discussion with the comment, "My experience has been that Hispanic girls don't want to go that far away from their home. So, will you apply to CSR [Cal State Riverside]?" Fortunately, Karen had brought along her mother's employer with her, a woman she referred to as her "mentor." The mentor corrected the counselor by stating that actually Karen was planning to apply to Harvard, Stanford, and Princeton. Karen recollected, "It is true that part of the Hispanic culture is that students tend to stay closer to their families. But, even though those stereotypes exist, they should not have that state of mind. They shouldn't be able to limit students like that."

Dominique, a young Black woman from South Central Los Angeles, for instance, remembered her experience, reporting, "Your parents did not go to college, no one in your family went to college. You have no idea what college is like and how hard it is to get in. Then someone tells you that you can't do it. You don't know what to think." The expectancies that adults like teachers and counselors hold and convey to young women have a direct influence on the expectancies that the students develop for themselves.

Physical Beauty as an Expectancy

The Rosenthal and Jacobson study and real-world stories from young women like Karen and Dominique make it clear that false expectations can influence how a perceiver, in these cases a teacher or counselor, behaves toward a target, in this case students. This biased behavior then can lead the target to act in a way that confirms the expectancy. Snyder, Tanke, and Berscheid (1977) conducted a study on expectations in a collegiate context. In their study, male students at the University of Minnesota were shown pictures of either an attractive or an unattractive woman, and were told that they would be talking on the telephone with the woman in the picture later in the study. Unbeknownst to the participants in the study, the male study participants did not actually speak to the people shown in the photographs. Instead, they spoke with a student who was selected randomly from a group of female student volunteers. So, as in Rosenthal and Jacobson's (1968) study, the expectancies were not correlated with the actual attractiveness of the women on the other end of the phone.

Snyder and his colleagues tape-recorded the telephone conversations between the men and their allegedly "attractive" or "unattractive" conversational partners. The phone conversations were analyzed on several dimensions. The results showed that when the men were under the impression that they were speaking with an attractive woman, the *women* who were the conversational partners actually ended up speaking more warmly than the women did when the men had been shown an unattractive photograph. Apparently, men who believed that they were speaking to an attractive woman brought out attractive behavior in the conversational partners, regardless of the conversational partners' actual physical appearances. Results from both the Rosenthal and Jacobson (1968) and the Snyder et al. studies suggest that our expectations play a rather large role in both how we react to other people, and in turn how they act toward us. Expectations have this effect regardless of whether they are objectively true, manipulated, or exist naturally in the environment. Believing a student to be a high performer is sufficient to bring about higher performance, and simply believing a person to be attractive is sufficient to bring about attractive behavior.

Expectancies in Black and White: Using Stereotypes to Form Expectancies

Can thoughts about gender, race, or ethnicity cause a self-fulfilling prophecy? The research we have discussed so far showed the power of expectancies that were clearly, but inaccurately, communicated to a person by a third party. We turn now to a consideration of whether an expectancy a person holds that is based solely on a target's membership in a racial group can also lead to self-fulfilling prophecy. Carl Word, Mark Zanna, and I conducted a study to look at this question (Word, Zanna, & Cooper, 1974). Would White college students' stereotypes about Black students lead to a self-fulfilling prophecy? Would the behavior of our students be unconsciously influenced by expectations they have of students of different races? And if stereotype-based expectancies ultimately cause Black target students to act differently, *how* are those expectancies communicated?

In our study, White university students were told that they would be working as a team with four other students to compete for a monetary prize. They were further told that the teams had been partially formed already, but that it would be necessary to select the final team member through an interview process. Each participant was told that he had been randomly selected to be the interviewer, and that he would select the team member out of a group of four candidates. What the participants did not know was that the researchers actually hired the ostensible job candidates and trained them to respond to the interview questions identically according to a carefully rehearsed script. Out of the four candidates, we were interested in the participants' behavior toward two of them. One of these key "team candidates" was Black; the other was White. Each interviewer interviewed one White and one Black candidate, and the order of the interviews was randomized. That is, some participants interviewed the White candidate first and the Black candidate second, and other participants interviewed the Black candidate first and the White candidate second. What we were really interested in investigating was how the behavior of the interviewers changed depending on expectancies they had about the race of the job candidates.

Results from the Word, Zanna, and Cooper (1974) study showed that although the Black and White job candidates answered the interviewers' questions in exactly the same way because they had spent equal time rehearsing the script, they were not treated equally by our interviewers. Videotapes of the sessions showed that interviewers spent 25% less time interviewing the Black candidates than they did interviewing the White candidates. Additionally, when addressing the White candidates, the interviewers used much more positive nonverbal behaviors in the interview—they sat closer to the White candidates than the Black candidates, and they made fewer speech errors when talking to the White candidates than when talking to the Black candidates. We interpreted the differences in these nonverbal behaviors to a difference in expectancies. Due to social stereotypes about different racial groups, White job interviewers may not have expected the Black candidates to be as qualified as the White candidates. The interviewers also may have expected to like the White candidates better than the Black candidates. Without consciously realizing what they were doing, the interviewers acted differently toward the candidates.

Does Differential Behavior Lead to a Self-Fulfilling Prophecy?

The study just described showed that the Black and White candidates were treated differently by the interviewers. However, was this differential behavior enough to instigate a self-fulfilling prophecy? That is, would the way the interviewers acted with the black candidates be sufficient to bring about poorer interview performance had the candidates not been confederates? We conducted a follow-up study to see if the types of behaviors exhibited by the interviewers toward the White and Black candidates in the first study would actually lead candidates to respond differently in the interviews. To test this, we needed to set up the situation such that the interviewers were now hired "confederates" trained to act either exactly as the interviewers in the first study did with the White candidates, or as they did with the Black candidates. We then wanted to see if the candidates' performance in the interviews was influenced by the way the interviewer had acted. For half of the candidates, the interviewers were instructed to act exactly as the interviewers in the first study had acted when they were talking to a White candidate. That is, they were instructed to sit a specified relatively close distance to the applicants, to make the interview longer, and to make relatively few speech errors. For the other half of the candidates, the interviewers were instructed to act exactly as the interviewers in the first study had acted toward Black candidates. That is, they were told to sit farther away from the candidates, to make the interview shorter, and to use more speech errors in the interview.

We videotaped the interviews, and had judges rate the candidates' interview performance on a number of dimensions. The results from this follow-up study showed that when the interview situation mirrored the situation experienced by the Black candidates in the first study, the job candidates were rated as less adequate for the job than they were when the interview situation mirrored that experienced by the White candidates in the first study. Relative to candidates who were treated as the Whites had been in the first study, candidates treated like the Blacks were also rated as being less calm and composed. Additionally, results showed that participants reciprocated the interpersonal distance set up by the interviewers. Those in the situation mirroring the Blacks' experience responded to the interviewers' large interpersonal distance by moving their chairs away an average of four inches. In contrast, those in the close interpersonal distance condition actually moved their chairs an average of eight inches closer to the interviewers. How did the candidates like the interviewers? We also asked the candidates questions about their perceptions of the interviewers when the sessions were completed. Compared to those who had been treated like the Whites had in the first study, candidates who had been in the condition set up to mirror the Blacks' experience reported that they thought their interviewers were significantly less friendly and significantly less adequate.

These results indicate, then, that stereotypes can lead to expectations. These expectations, in turn, lead to differential behavior by the "perceivers" which can actually lead to expectancy-consistent behavior by the targets. As a consequence of this complicated pattern of interactions, stereotypes can actually end up being confirmed, even if they are not true in objective reality. A well-qualified Black candidate, for instance, may perform poorly on an interview not because he or she is a bad candidate, but rather because he or she responds to an interviewer's interpersonal distance and negative nonverbal cues. When the target of the communication then reacts to such negative cues, it can be construed by the interviewer as evidence of incompetence and, for all appearances, the interviewer's original expectancy is confirmed.

SELF-FULFILLING PROPHECIES, GIRLS, AND COMPUTING

Research on expectancies and self-fulfilling prophecies speaks volumes about what girls are likely to experience while using computers in education. There are pervasive cultural stereotypes that girls do not enjoy or are not good at computers. It is very likely that these stereotypes influence how parents and teachers interact with girls when they use computers. Parents may encourage their boys to use computers but discourage their girls. More probably, parents act with benign neglect when girls approach computers. We know that parents indicate a greater willingness to spend money for computers for their sons than for their daughters and do, in fact, purchase more computers for their sons (Littleton et al., 1998). In school, teachers may pay more attention to the projects on which the boys are working, encourage boys more, and make more assumptions that the boys will be ready for more complicated tasks. As we saw in chapter 2, teachers may even merge their technology instruction with specialized knowledge of such traditionally male interests as football and baseball statistics (Schofield, 1995). The environment created by these expectancies is a major reason that girls begin to disidentify with the computer, feel less comfortable when using them, and become generally alienated from the computer culture.

Expectations and Attributions for Success and Failure

In addition to their role in self-fulfilling prophecies, our performance expectancies can also influence our self-perceptions. In this section, we discuss the role of gender expectancies and how they can influence the way in which people learn to explain to themselves the reasons for their success or failure at academic tasks. Psychologists know that the way people explain, or attribute, their success or failure at a task is an important determinant of their emotional reactions to that task, their future performance on tasks in that domain, and their predictions for how they will perform in the future. A girl who does well in her seventh-grade computer programming class has several possible explanations for her good performance. She can attribute her good performance to her intrinsic computer programming ability, and tell herself that she did well because she has a high aptitude in mathematical-like analytic reasoning. Alternatively, she can attribute her good performance to effort, and can tell herself that she did well in the course because she put a lot of time into the final project, or to luck, and tell herself that she was just fortunate about what items were on the exam.

Notice that although the intrinsic ability, the effort, and the luck explanations are effective in explaining to the student why she did well in the class, they have very different consequences for her predictions about her future performance in computer science courses. The intrinsic ability explanation makes rosy predictions about future performance in programming courses. The girl will feel confident in her ability, and will likely predict that she will also perform well in the next course she takes. In contrast, if the student attributes her success to a lot of hard work or to luck, predictions about future performance may not be as encouraging. The student may think to herself, "If I had to work so hard in this course, the next course may be even more difficult," or, "I may not be so fortunate next time."

Social psychologists have wrestled with the general question of how people make inferences on the basis of their performance. When a person performs well or poorly in any domain, not just on a computer task, how does the person decide what attribution to make about the performance? Moreover, how do those attributions help in making an inference about his or her ability based on that performance? One influential model of ability attribution was introduced by Bernard Weiner and his colleagues (e.g., Weiner, 1979; Weiner et al., 1971). Weiner's view suggests that people use performance to make two basic attributions: one about the stability of the performance over time, and the other about the locus of control of the performance. If Martha or Jared does well at a task, they first need to decide about locus of control for their performance—that is, were their performances controlled by internal or external factors? Internal factors include the children's ability and effort. External factors (i.e., things that neither Jared nor Martha could have controlled) include how difficult the task was and how lucky they may have been. If Jared did well because the task was easy or because he was simply lucky when he made wild guesses, then he will decide that his performance was dictated by events that were external to him. If Martha thinks she did well because she is smart or because she tried hard, then she will have decided that the control was internal to her rather than external.

And each child must also decide how stable the performance is likely to be. Perhaps Jared and Martha believe that their performance today is a good indicant of their performance tomorrow. If they failed today, they will typically fail. If they succeeded today, then they will typically succeed. Stable attributions can be based on the quality of the task or the ability of the person. For example, Martha might make a stable attribution if she believed that a particular IT program in her classroom was easy. She did well, and she would always do well on this task, because the program was particularly simple. If asked to take another quiz using that program, she would do well again. By contrast, Jared might make a stable attribution using a different route. He might decide that he was simply good at IT tasks. Jared could reason that his superior ability in IT would make him succeed at virtually any computer task that the teacher could present to him. Like the seventh-grade student in the preceding example, this would instill Jared with great confidence as he moves from task to task.

According to Weiner et al. (1971), when each of us succeeds or fails at a task, we go through the inference steps that Jared and Martha went through. The basic pattern of attributional possibilities are shown in Figs. 4.1 and 4.2.

It is a great advantage for our self-esteem and for our willingness to pursue challenging opportunities if we make internal *and* stable attributions for our success and *either* an external *or* unstable attribution for our failures. If we believe that our success is an indicant of our ability (the internal, stable attribution), we are more psychologically prepared and confident to pursue challenging extensions in the domain in which we have already succeeded. However, if we make a stable, internal attribution after we fall short on a task, then the likelihood that we will persevere is diminished. Simply put, if we think our performance tells us that we have little or no

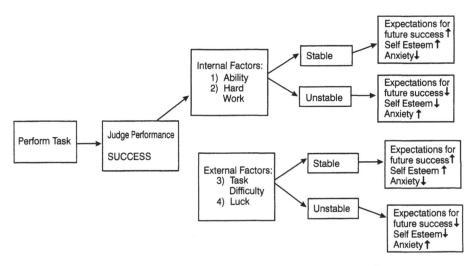

FIG. 4.1. Attributional stages when outcome judged as a success (adapted from Weiner, 1986).

ability in a particular domain in life, we are unlikely to continue to pursue it. When children make errors at a school task, it is more adaptive to conclude that this particular iteration of the task was difficult, or they were just unlucky, or they didn't try hard enough. Any of those attributions allows the child to consider the possibility that he or she has the ability to succeed on some future instance that requires this ability. Weiner and his colleagues have provided considerable evidence that people who attribute success at

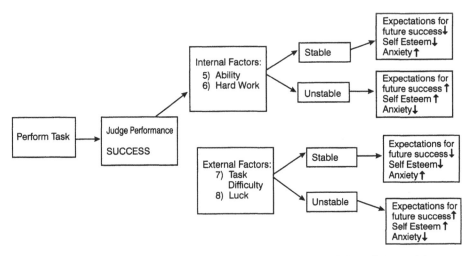

FIG. 4.2. Attributional stages when outcome judged as a failure (adapted from Weiner, 1985).

a particular task to the internal, stable factor of ability experience their success as rewarding and are more likely to approach the task again. Individuals who attribute failure to lack of effort are likely to persist and increase their efforts in the face of failure, whereas individuals who attribute failure to lack of ability are likely to give up in face of failure and avoid such tasks in the future.

Martha and Jared are not on a level playing field when it comes to making attributions for success and failure in achievement-related tasks. Several research studies have shown that males and females often provide different attributions for success and failure in achievement situations (Deaux, 1976; Dweck & Reppucci, 1973; Frieze, 1976; Nicholls, 1975; Nelson & Cooper, 1997). In a study of fifth-grade children, Nicholls (1975) found that girls showed a pattern he described as "self-derogating." They attributed failure to ability more than they attributed success to ability, and they attributed success to luck more than they attributed failure to luck. Boys, on the other hand, showed a pattern that Nicholls termed "self-enhancing." In contrast to the girls, boys attributed failure to luck more than they attributed success to luck and concluded that success was simply a function of their superior ability.

Carol Dweck and her colleagues found a similar pattern of results (e.g., Licht & Dweck, 1984). She has reasoned that, in comparison to girls, boys are "mastery oriented." They attribute success to high ability and failure to bad luck or an unfair evaluator. Girls show a pattern of "learned helplessness," attributing their failures to lack of ability and their successes to chance, luck, or task difficulty. Diener and Dweck (1978) found that children who were characterized by learned helplessness attributions were more likely to experience negative emotions after failure at a task and then engage in numerous ineffective strategies as the task progressed. Mastery-oriented children blamed failure on a combination of effort, luck, and unfairness. They experienced more positive emotions and engaged in increasingly effective, useful strategies as the task progressed.

Why do some children and adults tend to favor one type of attribution over the other? And why is gender one of the primary factors that divide people into mastery orientation and learned helplessness? The phenomenon is especially clear when technological fields including mathematics are the focus of attention. Even when children have equal abilities as measured by standardized test scores and course grades, girls show greater tendencies to make the helpless, self-derogating attributions for their performance and boys tend to show the self-enhancing, mastery orientation. One major influence on children's attributional patterns comes from parental influence, almost certainly unintentionally. Parents are interpreters of reality for their children. They help children learn about their relationship to the world. Although they are not the only influence, they are the first interpreters of the world, and information they provide sets the stage for all future influences. Parents are not immune to the social stereotypes that permeate society. Therefore, it is not surprising that parents' gender stereotypes and expectancies affect the performance attributions that they communicate to their children.

How do children generate the explanation for their own performance in areas such as information technology, science and mathematics? Much of the research and theorizing on this question has been focused on gender and mathematics, but the concepts are relevant to IT as well. Parsons, Meece, Adler, and Kaczala (1982) suggested that parents may act as "expectancy socializers." They communicate to children what they think of their children's abilities. Although they may not be aware of it, parents hold many of the gender expectancies about their children's abilities and interest in mathematics that are consistent with society's stereotypes, and they will inadvertently communicate their expectations to their children. Parsons and her colleagues asked parents and students to respond to several questionnaire items. Students were asked to rate their own math ability, their perceptions of the effort they needed to make to do well in math, and the difficulty of their current math course. Parents were also asked questions to assess their beliefs and attitudes about their children. They responded to questionnaire items asking them to rate their children's math ability, their perceptions of the effort their child must make to do well in math, their expectations for their child's future math performance, and their perceptions of how difficult math courses are for the child. In addition to these questionnaire items, Parsons et al. also obtained objective measures from each student's academic record of their grades in math courses as well as their scores on standardized test scores.

Results from this study showed that there were no differences at all between boys and girls in either their math grades or in their performance on the standardized tests. However, despite the striking similarities in math performance between boys and girls, parents' estimates of their child's math ability was significantly influenced by the sex of the child. In particular, results showed that parents of daughters were more likely than parents of sons to feel that math was more difficult for their child, and that it was necessary for their child to put forth a lot of effort in math courses in order to do well.

It is, of course, possible that the boys and girls did put forth different amounts of effort to obtain the same grades, and that parents' answers to the questionnaire items did reflect reality. Other research, however, has suggested that this is not the case. In fact, several studies have shown that although compared to boys, girls consistently report that they must exert more effort to do well in math, objective measures of actual homework time shows that girls and boys are putting forth equivalent time studying for math courses. Parsons et al. argue that parents' gender expectancies lead them to communicate to girls the message that they are doing well in math courses *because* they are exerting a lot of effort, and that this message leads the girls to attribute their good performance to effort.

The responses from the parents and students confirmed another important aspect of the "expectancy socializer" hypothesis. Parsons et al. found that parental attitudes about their daughters' mathematics ability *caused* the differences in how the daughters interpreted their success at mathematics. Girls' self-concept about their mathematics ability was more highly related to their parents' attitudes than it was to their own past performance. If girls did well in mathematics, they were unlikely to attribute their success to their ability in math and more likely to attribute their success to plain hard work—if that is what their parents believe. And the more strongly the parents say they expect that their daughters will have to work hard in order to succeed, the more likely the daughter will believe that explanation rather than believing they are actually good in math. The reasons for success or failure on tasks are usually ambiguous or multi-determined. A student rarely knows how much time the other students in the class are spending on their homework. Because of this inherent ambiguity, if parents expect that girls need to try harder than boys to perform well at math, and communicate this expectancy to their daughters, the daughters come to attribute their performance to hard work rather than to their own natural ability. Girls and boys may then come to explain what is in actuality identical performance and effort to different reasons.

In a recent study on a similar topic, Tiedemann (2000) also looked at the relationship between objective measures of mathematical ability, children's perceptions of their own math ability, and parents' perceptions of the children's math ability in a study of 589 elementary school students. Like Parsons et al., Tiedemann (2000) found that, overall, both mothers and fathers were more likely to think that boys are more skilled in mathematics than girls. What is striking is that, as in Parson's study, the parents reported these gender-biased performance expectations even though there were no objective or actual performance differences in math between the boys and the girls in the sample.

Tiedemann (2000) also found that the parents' gender-stereotypic beliefs exerted an independent influence on their perceptions of their children's abilities. In other words, parents with more gender-stereotypic beliefs about math ability were more likely to judge their sons as having higher abilities than their daughters. In turn, the parents' beliefs about the ability of their sons and daughters influenced the children's self-perceptions of their own math ability.

The results from both the Parsons et al. and Tiedemann studies suggest that children's self-perceptions of their own math abilities are influenced by the degree to which their parents have knowledge of or "buy into" the prevailing stereotypes about girls' mathematical competence. These studies also highlight how subtle these expectancies can be. From these studies, we can conclude that one of the ways parents' math ability stereotypes exert their effect is by influencing *how* children explain their successes and failures in mathematics.

PERFORMANCE ATTRIBUTIONS AND INFORMATION TECHNOLOGY

The study of gender differences in mathematics has had a far longer research history than its counterpart in the field of computers. The issues, however, are similar. If parents believe that computers are more appropriate for their sons than their daughters or if teachers believe that the boys in their classes will outperform the girls on computer tasks, then those expectancies will have direct consequences on both computer anxiety and the attributions that girls and boys make for their successes and failure. Parents who wittingly or unwittingly accept the gender stereotype that women are not as good as men at computers may inadvertently communicate to their daughters that any good performance on computer-related tasks is not due to their innate aptitude for analytical reasoning and computer programming, but rather due to the work and effort they put into the task. That is the theory. We conducted a research project to see if it was true (Nelson & Cooper, 1997).

Our study took place in a rural section of central New Jersey. Fifth-grade boys and girls from public and parochial schools comprised the participant group. Our study had three major goals. The first was to assess students' attitudes and stereotypes about computers. The second was to determine the attributions boys and girls make when succeeding or failing with information technology. The third was to determine what the consequences of succeeding and failing at an IT task actually are for boys and for girls. Would success encourage children? Would failure dishearten them and cause them to abandon IT? Would gender make a difference?

The children filled out a questionnaire about their reactions to computers. As has been found by many other investigators, boys felt more competent using IT than did girls. When we examined our data to find out why this was true, we found that the effect was mediated by two factors: prior experience and belief in the gender stereotype. The more experience a child had, the more positive his or her attitude was toward the computer. But, even at age 10, boys had far more experience with computers than did girls. The differential access to computers early in life seemed to translate into differential feelings of competence by the fifth grade. Boys felt more competent than girls.

We also found that children endorsed the stereotype about gender and computers. They believed that the use of a computer was significantly more a male domain than a female domain. Interestingly, this was a position particularly endorsed by the boys. Nonetheless, neither the boys nor the girls thought that computers were part of the female domain. For boys and for girls, perceived competence was affected by the stereotype. The more boys thought that IT was part of the male domain, the more competence and confidence they expressed. For girls, the pattern was reversed. The more they endorsed the male stereotype, the less confident and competent they felt.

Attributions for Success and Failure

Have you ever used an IT program that crashed on you? Have you ever had a piece of software deliver a cryptic error message, implying that some dire event had occurred and the computer would not do what you asked it to do? Most of us have had such failures in our interactions with computers. We wanted to assess how boys and girls would attribute such failures so we devised a situation that ensured that our 10-year-olds would have one. Or, they would have a success experience, depending on the condition to which they were randomly assigned.

Several weeks after they filled out their IT questionnaire, we contacted the children again in their elementary schools and asked them to perform an anagrams task. Generally, children like to unscramble letters, and they eagerly agreed to participate (parental permission had previously been obtained, of course.) Each child was tested alone, without the presence of any other students. Seated in front of their computer screen, the child saw the message, "Welcome to anagrams" and was given brief instructions about how to use the program. The experimenter summarized the instructions verbally, pointed out the <Return> key, and explained how to edit mistakes.

The children had 11 anagrams to unscramble, all of which were relatively easy for the fifth graders. We wanted the children to experience success or failure *at the computer* and not at the anagrams task. Consequently, as children in the "failure condition" proceeded through the task, they occasionally found that those nasty error messages that characterize some of the experiences we all have had with the computer. On the very first trial, a child in the failure condition would unscramble the letters *b, k, o,* and *o* and write the word *book*. The computer then revealed that the child was correct, then displayed the message, "$bus error; core dumped!!!WARNING ON DRIVE 788*9x)." The student was instructed to wait while the experimenter fixed the machine. Similar error messages occurred after the fifth, seventh, ninth, and eleventh trials, with the final message reading, "system going down IMMEDIATELY. 39% errors using machine!" All the while, the student received accurate feedback on his or her anagram performance.

In the "success" condition, the computer cooperated marvelously. It simply gave feedback to the student on the anagram task. At the end, the child read, "No user errors detected. Thank you." In all conditions, students were given a questionnaire designed to assess how they attributed their performance. The results for success and failure were dramatically affected by gender. When the computer spewed out error messages, only 6% of the boys attributed their lack of success to their ability. Fifty percent thought that if they tried harder, they would not have made computer errors. For girls, however, the percentage that thought their ability accounted for their failure rose to 19%, with effort attributions accounting for only 31%.

In the "success" conditions, boys took credit for their ability much more than girls did. As Fig. 4.3 shows, 29% of the boys, but only 5% of the girls attributed success on the IT program to their ability. Ninety-five percent of the girls thought that they had either worked hard to attain the success, were lucky, or had an easy task.

CONSEQUENCES OF THE ATTRIBUTIONS: THE "SO WHAT?" QUESTION

We have maintained that making stable, internal attributions for success is adaptive and causes children to feel competent to pursue computer tasks more frequently. We have also maintained that making such attributions for failure is less adaptive, causes negative emotions, and leads to abandoning technology on future tasks. In the Nelson and Cooper (1997) exper-

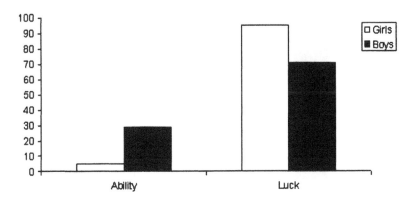

FIG. 4.3. Percentage of girls and boys attributing their success on the IT task to ability versus luck. Adapted from Nelson & Cooper, 1997, Gender differences in children's reactions to success and failure with computers. *Computers in Human Behavior, 13,* 247–267, copyright © 1997, with permission from Elsevier.

iment, we asked the children the "so what?" question. Do differential attributions matter to them in terms of their taking on IT tasks in the future?

When the children were finished with their anagrams task, they were asked: If they were given the chance to use a different program to learn anagrams, did they think they would use it effectively? There was no difference between boys and girls who had succeeded on the prior IT task. However, there was a significant gender difference in the "failure" condition. Girls, who had been much more likely to attribute failure to their lack of ability with computers, were far less likely than boys to think that they would do well on a subsequent computer program.

Students also showed that the attributional styles for failure and for success protected boys' self-confidence about computer use. Asked how they perceived their ability with computers compared to the ability of others of the same age, the boys were overwhelmingly positive, regardless of whether they succeeded or failed. Girls who succeeded at our task thought that their ability was about average, whereas girls who had been in the "failure" condition thought that their ability was significantly less than that of the average fifth grader. These results are depicted in Fig. 4.4.

We then gave the students a chance to "vote with their feet." We had one more academic task for them. They met a different experimenter at their schools who told them, "You will now be playing a word game called 'Rhymes.' You can either do it on the computer or you can do it with paper and pencil. It doesn't matter which one you choose, but you need to choose one or the other. Which do you want to do?"

The students who had made stable, internal attributions for their success (mostly the boys), wanted to use the computer to do the Rhymes task.

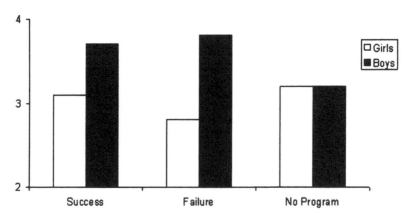

FIG. 4.4. Perceived ability relative to other students depending on whether student had succeeded or failed on previous task. Adapted from Nelson & Cooper, 1997, Gender differences in children's reactions to success and failure with computers. *Computers in Human Behavior, 13*, 247–267, copyright © 1997, with permission from Elsevier.

Those who had made effort or luck attributions were more likely to want to use paper and pencil. Similarly, students who had been in the "failure" condition and who had decided that their stable ability was the source of their failure (mostly the girls) were less likely to want to use the computer, opting for the pencil-and-paper version instead.

The cycle is a vicious one, continually spiraling toward greater anxiety and disidentification for females. Gender stereotypes result in a pattern of attributions that make self-confidence very difficult and make computer anxiety very likely. If girls do have successful experiences with technology, it is due to luck or effort; if girls have an unsuccessful experience, it is a reflection of their (lack of) ability. As our research reveals, girls believe these explanations, making it difficult to approach a subsequent technology interaction with confidence. The lack of confidence in their own ability fosters and amplifies computer anxiety, discouraging girls from enthusiastically taking on challenges that would increase their technological skills. Computers are not used; classes are avoided. In a study of students enrolled in an introductory computer science class at a New Jersey community college, Nelson, Weise, and Cooper (1991) found that computer anxiety predicted which female students were most likely to drop out of the course. The higher the initial computer anxiety, the more likely the students were to drop out. The same relationship was not found for male students. Males with anxiety about computers were actually more likely to pursue the course to its conclusion. The invidious consequence of gender-based computer anxiety is that fewer girls and women persevere. The gender imbalance is perpetuated, girls and women receive less instruction and experience, and the road to success in technology for women becomes all the more difficult.

EDUCATIONAL COMPUTER SOFTWARE: BOY-TALK PRODUCED BY GENDER EXPECTATIONS

We have argued that gender-biased expectancies can lead to self-fulfilling prophecies and can contribute to the types of attributions children learn to make for their performance on academic tasks. We now turn to a discussion of the role of expectancies in computer software design. As we discussed in chapter 2, a large proportion of IT programs appear to be written in "boy-talk." That is, to the dismay of most girls, they are designed with the features that boys rather than girls prefer. In light of this disparity, it seems reasonable to ask the question, *why do software manufacturers produce software that seems counterproductive to half the population?*

One answer, and not an incorrect one, is that the preponderance of software writers are male. Males produce what interests them and, as we have seen, the kinds of formal features in software that appeal to males include space and war metaphors, competition, eye-hand coordination tasks, and the like. It is quite likely that each of us would have a tendency to produce creative material that is to our own liking and, thus, male creators of educational software tend to produce software that they would have enjoyed using while they were in school. Teachers, being professionally trained, might be in a better position to refrain from making all of their own biases and preferences the springboard for their classroom lessons. However, software creators are not usually teachers. Their skill generally lies in program design and code writing. If they have a particular metaphor that they think would have motivated them to learn spelling, math, or music, they are likely to place such metaphors in the programs they are writing.

A second explanation, and one that we believe is extremely pervasive, is based on the unwitting expectations of the software designers. Just as a novelist, a musician, or a screenplay writer envisions the potential audience to which he or she is communicating as he or she creates artistic works, when a programmer sits down to write code or design a computer interface, he or she is writing to an audience. The software creator is communicating to another person just as the job interviewer communicated to the candidate in the Word et al. (1974) study or the male college students communicated to the female students in the experiment by Snyder et al. (1977).

When the software writer sits down to write a program to help children learn, what audience comes to his or her mind? Some research has shown that when people are asked to imagine the "typical" member of certain social categories, they are often gender-biased in their imaginings. For example, Miller, Taylor, and Buck (1991) asked a group of Princeton University students to spend a few minutes imagining the "typical American voter." These participants were then asked to answer questions about the age, marital status, and home state of the imagined voter. Some participants were also asked to indicate the gender of the person whom they had imagined. Results showed that despite the fact that the number of men and women voters is equal in the United States (in fact, there are slightly more women than men that are of voting age), the students were overwhelmingly more likely to describe the typical American voter as a male than a female. Seventy-two percent of the Princeton University students in the study indicated that the person they had imagined was male, whereas only 28% indicated that the person they had imagined was female. The results also showed that males and females were equally susceptible to this gender bias.

Other studies have replicated the finding that often it is men that spring to mind when people are asked to describe the typical member of what are in reality gender-balanced groups. Eagly and Kite (1987) asked a group of college students to rate either the percentage of *women* in a given nationality, the percentage of *men* in a given nationality, or the percentage of *people* in a given nationality that possessed a series of attributes. Results showed that the students' ratings of the *people* in the nationality were more similar to their ratings of the men than they were to their ratings of the women. These results indicate that when thinking of the "people" in a given national group, students were more likely to have men spring to mind than women.

We thought that it was important to investigate this question in the context of educational software design. In addition to the tendency to see males as overrepresented in the population, the problem in software design is compounded by gender stereotypes. The association of boys with computers is so strong and pervasive that it establishes the expectation in the programmer that males rather than females will be the ones using the computer. We would also argue that this expectation is not necessarily a conscious one. In fact, if asked directly, we think that a programmer of educational software would surely acknowledge that only half of the potential classroom users are male, just like the Princeton students in Miller et al.'s (1991) study of the "typical American voter" would surely acknowledge that there are an equal number of male and female voters in the United States if they were asked directly.

However, despite the potential for this conscious realization, we hypothesized that the programmer sees himself or herself as creating a communication that is then transmitted through the interface of the computer to a boy sitting at his computer screen. The invidiousness of expectancy phenomena is that people do not think about it deliberately or consciously. It invades the subtlety of their thought processes and finds its way into the communicative act. As a consequence of his or her implicit expectation, the programmer thus engages in "boy-talk." The programmer writes in a way that he or she believes boys will appreciate. To motivate the boy, write about sports, space, or war. Encourage competition and add all the bells and whistles in your repertoire. However, the dilemma is that the IT software that ends up on the boys' and the girls' computers will be written in boy-talk, not an altogether pleasant experience for the girls.

Testing the Expectancy Communication Link

Chuck Huff and I set out to test these predictions (Huff & Cooper, 1987). We contacted school teachers in the state of New Jersey and asked them to help us in our research project. With the cooperation of the state's teachers' union, the New Jersey Education Association, we located a group of teachers who were members of a subgroup within NJEA committed to using computers in the classroom. This group, known as CLUES, was comprised of teachers from across the state representing the diverse geographic, demographic, and socioeconomic groupings that comprise the country's ninth most populous state.

We sent a letter to each teacher within CLUES, asking if they would help us with our study of computer use in schools. We received positive responses from 75 teachers. Seventy of the responses were from female teachers, so Huff and I made the decision to use only female teachers in our study. At the very least, this would eliminate whatever consequence there is of males writing the computer software.

We told each teacher that we wanted her to help us design a computer-assisted software program that would help children with one aspect of their studies. We selected an issue from English grammar. We asked them to help us design computer software that would help with the "appropriate use of commas." Why commas? We did not want the teachers to think of a program that they might have seen on the commercial market and allow that to influence the program they designed for our project. Perhaps it is a commentary on the importance that grammar plays in the curricula of classrooms at the start of the 21st century, but, to our knowledge, there are no currently available programs to educate students on the use of commas. For research purposes, this allowed us to be certain that the programs would be created by the ingenuity of the teachers.

We stressed to the teachers that we were asking them to "design" a program, not write computer code. Our interest was in what the teachers thought should appear on the screen, what the task of the student would be, how the student would interface with the task (e.g., pressing computer keys, using joy sticks), whether there would be light or sound or color. In the study, teachers were asked to answer some questions that were relevant to designing the program. They were asked to specify the theme of the program, how the child would interact with the task, how the student would know if his or her response was correct or not, what kinds of sound, color, or action would be incorporated into the program, and other relevant questions.

Unbeknownst to the teachers, there were three different sets of instructions used in the study. The difference in the instructions the teachers received was the key variable we were interested in studying. One group of teachers was asked, "What we would like you to do is design a computer program to teach seventh-grade *boys* the proper use of commas." Another group was given a very similar instruction but asked to design the program to teach commas to seventh-grade *girls*. By using this difference in instruction, we could systematically vary the target of the teacher's communicative act. Teachers in the first group knew that they were communicating specifically to seventh-grade boys. Teachers in the second group knew they were communicating to seventh-grade girls. Did their computer programs differ? Did they design programs using language, metaphors, and formal features that are liked by their respective audiences?

The answer is a resounding yes. Teachers wrote very different programs, depending on whether they anticipated boys or girls would be learning from the program. Let's first consider the computer program that teachers designed for boys. The programs were an ideal match for what we know boys prefer in computer software. Often, the commas were taught in a game-like atmosphere. Often, the games featured sport or war metaphors. Typically, teachers built in competition as an essential feature of the learning enterprise. The teachers went out of their way to tell us how the boys would be using joysticks and other accoutrements usually associated with games in the video arcade.

Consider some examples: Maryanne Smith, a middle school teacher, wrote an IT lesson for seventh-grade boys. Like all of the respondents, Ms. Smith was asked several questions. First, she was asked what the *theme* of the lesson is. "A sports game," was her response.

How will the child interact with the program? "With a joystick," she responded.

What will the child see on the screen of the computer? She described what would happen in the lesson this way: "Bursts of light [will be used] for correct answers. The game will use sports information. If commas are used incorrectly, the child must correct them. If the child responds correctly, a burst of light will appear. If the child is incorrect, the sentence explodes. An additional feature is that the player places a comma into the sentence with a cannon. He shoots them into place."

Finally, Ms. Smith was asked to write a brief description of the IT program, one that might be used in an advertisement or on a CD jacket to help a parent or a teacher to decide whether to purchase it. This is the description she wrote: "Here is an opportunity for your child to enjoy the world of sports and learn English grammar at the same time. Your child will enjoy shooting cannons and competing for the highest score. After playing with this program, your child will use commas in a natural and correct manner."

Now, consider the program written by another teacher in CLUES. Ms. Alicia Johnson had been asked to write a comma program for seventh-grade girls. It will be immediately apparent that Ms. Johnson avoids all of the features of IT that are associated with the male stereotype and, instead, incorporates the features more typically associated with a female stereotype. Here are some of her answers.

Theme: "A trip to the record shop."

What kind of sound, color or action might there be? "Color on the edges of the screen. A tune could be used for each comma rule."

What will the child see on the screen of the computer? "Children will be seen going to a record shop. They will see typed conversation between the two children. For example, Child #1 says to Child #2, '(Name), do you think we can find the record we want in this shop?' These sentences have to be punctuated by the pupil. If the answer is incorrect, a tutorial could be used to give the rule. The tutorial will be clear, use the pupil's name, and will be presented in words."

Description for an advertisement or CD jacket: "Two girls go on a shopping trip to a record shop to find music for a dance being given at their school. They 'converse' with each other and make decisions about what to buy. The use of commas and rules involved are taught through this trip. Reinforcement is available in worksheet form."

There is little doubt, from glancing at these two typical responses, that teachers have an excellent, intuitive idea of what boys and girls like, and are able to design a computer program that incorporated these elements into it. Ms. Smith's program, written with boys in mind, emphasizes the fast-paced game that seems like it jumped off the machines at the local video arcade. Sound, lights, and explosions accompany the sport metaphor as the target skill, commas, are shot into place. Ms. Johnson, writing with female users in mind, is more keenly aware that the user wants to learn the use of commas and therefore provides a clear, written tutorial. Her story line wraps her learning in a shopping metaphor, featuring communication and conversation. Expecting her target audience to be female, Ms. Johnson has written the perfect program. Similarly, Ms. Smith has written an ideal program to involve boys in the computer task.

The critical feature of the Huff and Cooper study was a comparison of the two conditions just described, with a third condition. We asked another group of teachers to design a program for seventh-grade *students* without specifying whether the students would be male or female. Who was in the mind's eye of a teacher writing for "students"? By systematically comparing the program written for students with programs written for boys and for girls, we can infer the degree to which the program authors (i.e., the teachers) unwittingly thought they were writing programs for boys, girls, or, as implied in the task, of mix of boys and girls. Results from this condition were so startling that they did not require subtle inferences. Teachers writing programs for *students* wrote programs almost identical to the programs written for boys. Consider the following example, taken from the responses of Ms. Adrianne Shea, as she described her comma program:

Theme: "The program would be a game. It should be a fast arcade-type game."

What will the child see on the screen of the computer? "Arcade-type sounds should accompany a hit (correct response) and 'burbling' sounds should be coordinated with the score counter ... Correct hits should result in wild color displays. Action should involve marquee moving sentences which, if correctly punctuated, are shot off the screen, using the space bar."

Description for an Advertisement or CD jacket: "Here's a fast-paced program for your arcade game lovers. Just what the teenager spends his quarters on! It's also a program teachers will welcome. It provides your students with the practice they need to recognize the correct use of commas. Sentences zip across the screen—some correctly punctuated with commas, some not. Correct sentences are 'zapped' off the screen by your students as they try to be on the roster of top scorers."

Competition, shooting, action, zapping, this program truly has it all—if you are a boy. The gender-based expectancy for the child on the receiving end of the computer program is clearly a boy. Ms. Shea has tailored her IT communication to the prototypical boy rather than finding a combination of interests implied by the instructions to communicate the use of commas to all students. Ms. Shea was by no means alone in her response.

Figure 4.5 presents the results of a multi-dimensional scaling conducted on the data from all 75 teachers who wrote IT programs. This statistical technique is designed to graph the elements of the computer programs onto a dimension. It shows how similar and different the typical programs are in each condition. On the top panel, we see the program for boys. The arrow demonstrates the central tendency for this game on a dimension that runs from being very much like an arcade game to being more like a learning tool. The arrow in the top panel shows that, like Ms. Smith's description, the average teacher wrote IT programs for boys that were heavily weighted on the game side. By contrast, the average program written for girls was very different, with the central tendency arrow all the way on the other side of the scale. The third panel shows the scaling for the "students" program. Indeed, it is virtually a carbon copy of the top panel—that is, the program written for boys.

We have seen how communications can be unwittingly altered to match the stereotypes people have about the target of their communications. In the Word et al. study, college students communicated their negative expectations about African American students such that African Americans performed more poorly at an interview and felt worse about themselves. In the current study, well-meaning teachers communicated to girls that IT was not for them, but rather for boys. Although they proved quite capable of communicating to girls when they were asked to think specifically of female students, they clearly were communicating with boys when simply asked to think of

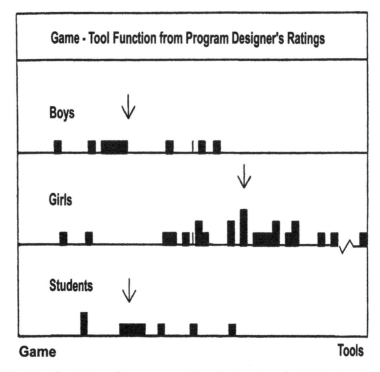

FIG. 4.5.   Depiction of programs written by teachers for instructing boys (top panel), girls (middle panel), and students (lower panel) the use of commas. The arrow in each panel depicts the central tendency of each group along dimensions of games versus learning tools. Reprinted with permission from *Journal of Applied Social Psychology, Vol 17*, number 6, pp. 519–532. Copyright © by V. H. Winston & Son, Inc., 360 South Ocean Boulevard, Palm Beach, FL 33480. All rights reserved.

students in general. These nonconscious expectancies are yet another factor convincing girls that computer technology is not for them. They are communications directed at and for boys. The consequence of girls having to learn from communications that were not constructed with them in mind is surely a further disidentification with the very technology that is supposed to help them learn.

5

A Threat in the Air

The digital divide between males and females is very real and very damaging. It is damaging for women who will have to combat more than a few barriers to achieve comfort with information technology. It is damaging for society, because half of the potential workforce must fight an uphill battle to contribute to the creative process in IT. Most women who have an interest in information technology drop out. Those who stay the course have a difficult time taking their place in the higher echelons of the workforce. If Martha is to take her place alongside Jared as someone who is comfortable and knowledgeable with computers, she will have to overcome most of the obstacles that we have examined in this book. She will have to use computers in school, despite IT software that makes her feel uncomfortable. When she reaches the psychological stage of gender constancy, Martha will incorporate society's ideas of computers as boy-toys, not girl-toys, into her own self-concept of what it means for her to be a girl. Typically, computer lessons in school will be conducted in a social context that will exacerbate her anxiety and render outstanding performance more difficult. Later, she may have to endure her parents and other adults teaching her to attribute her successes in IT, mathematics, or science to luck while attributing failures to her lack of ability.

Year after year, Martha will be bombarded with these forces. They will be applied subtly and mostly unwittingly by the adults and peers in her environment. In the end, Martha will likely conclude that she simply is not good at IT, math, or science, that she is not interested in these subjects anyway, and that she would expect not to be terribly good at any new task that required skill and comfort with computers. In short, there will be extreme pressure for Martha to come to believe that she cannot succeed at information technology. Such expectations typically transform themselves into reality, with a resounding loss for Martha and for society.

We have presented a case for the prototypical girl. Despite the best intentions of her teachers and parents, we believe that Martha will have a difficult time persevering with information technology or feeling good about her ability in this male-oriented domain. But there are many girls who will face all of the pressures society has to offer and still believe that they are as capable as boys in these masculine-stereotyped fields. They can handle computers, solve their mathematics problems and conduct their science projects. Such girls are aware of the societal stereotypes, but they have not incorporated them. They may have had parents and teachers who, unlike the adults in typical families, taught them that they had more than enough ability to pursue any subject matter or career choice that involved technology. They may have had teachers who searched diligently for IT software that was gender neutral rather than male oriented. They may have had a nurturing environment that fostered a sense of self-esteem and competence that transcended all of the traps that society threw in their way.

In chapter 3, we reported that when children were asked whether boys or girls are better at using computers, not a single child chose girls as the superior sex for computer ability. When students made choices, they always picked boys. However, a large proportion of the girls thought that neither gender was superior or inferior with computers. These girls either did not believe the stereotype that boys are better at computers than girls or they did not believe that the stereotype applied to them. Despite all of the pitfalls, Martha may fully believe that *she* is as competent with computer tasks as boys, despite the stereotypical general superiority of boys over girls at information technology.

If Martha believes that she is different from the stereotype—either because the stereotype is not true or because she feels she has more ability at information technology than the average girl—will she still suffer the deleterious effects of those stereotypes? Research in social psychology suggests that, despite her impressive resistance to the social stereotype, Martha will nonetheless be subjected to pressures that will reduce her performance and that may lead her, in the end, to distance herself from computer technology. We refer, here, to the phenomenon of *stereotype threat*.

STEREOTYPE THREAT: THE DIGITAL DIVIDE AND THE STEREOTYPE

Claude Steele, Joshua Aronson, and their colleagues (e.g., Spencer, Steele, & Quinn, 1999; Steele, 1997; Steele & Aronson, 1995) focused the research spotlight on this fascinating and important topic. They argued that, under the proper circumstances, the mere existence and knowledge of a negative stereotype causes anxiety and pressure in members of the stereotyped group. If women know that they are considered inferior in their math, science, or computer abilities, they are confronted with a predicament. They know that observers (e.g., teachers, employers, males) possess this stereotype and will use it as a lens through which their performance will be judged.

Let us imagine that a female college student is taking a computer programming quiz in front of her professor. She feels she is quite capable of being one of the better students in her class, regardless of gender. That is, this student has not accepted the stereotype as applying to her. Nonetheless, she is also aware that her professor knows the women-can't-understand-computers stereotype. She fears being judged by that stereotype. She wants desperately to disconfirm it. She keenly feels the pressure to succeed, but is equally aware that any slip-up may confirm her professor's stereotype. She is in the throes of a dilemma characterized by fear of appearing to confirm the stereotype and a pressure to succeed. Performing well in this dilemma is difficult indeed. The psychological demands on her are far greater than merely applying her skills to the test. The weight of being judged by the negative stereotype rests heavily on her shoulders. She is likely to succumb to the double dose of pressure and anxiety. Precisely because she is so intent on disconfirming the negative stereotype, she is likely to deliver a performance that confirms it. It is not a dilemma faced by the males in the class.

Stereotype threat is not unique to computer skills. It exists any time there is a negative stereotype about a group, and a group member has the expectation of being judged by that stereotype. The White male on a basketball team in a mostly Black high school may fear that his first missed layup will be taken as a sign that Whites are not adequate basketball players. Perhaps he should not take a shot. If he doesn't, he will confirm the stereotype. If he does, and misses, he will confirm the stereotype. The African American student in the classroom may worry that any failure to raise his hand in response to a question will be taken as a confirmation of laziness or a lack of intelligence. On the other hand, a single incorrect answer to a teacher's question may lead to the same confirmation. The pressure on him mounts. A woman in a math class similarly suffers. She knows the stereotype, knows that it is held by her teacher and other students in the class. She suffers the anxiety and pressure that come from the need to disconfirm the stereotype and the constant fear of being judged by it. Neither the White basketball player nor the African American student nor the female math student needs to believe that the stereotype applies to him or her. The stereotype is "in the air" and will do its damage.

Race and Stereotype Threat

The first empirical test of stereotype threat was conducted by Steele and Aronson (1995). Racial identity was the basis for the stereotype, and performance on a difficult academic test was used as the criterion to examine the consequence of stereotype threat on African American students. Steele and Aronson argued that the stereotype of African Americans that typically includes a belief in poor academic performance would lead Black students to underperform on the test relative to Whites. Steele and Aronson also reasoned that Black students would be affected by the stereotype *if* they believed that the test was somehow diagnostic of their abilities. If not, then stereotypes about their ability would not impact on test performance. Put another way, if students thought that they were playing a game that happened to have some academic questions on it but those questions had nothing to do with their abilities as students, they would not be worried about whether or not they confirmed the negative stereotypes. Students who answered the same questions, but thought that the score was an indicator of their scholastic ability, would feel the pressure and anxiety of stereotype threat.

Black and White college women were recruited for the research. Those randomly placed in the diagnostic condition were told that the test they were about to take "may be helpful to you by familiarizing you with some of your strengths and weaknesses" and described it as "a genuine test of your verbal abilities and limitations." In the nondiagnostic condition, participants were simply assured that "we're not going to evaluate your ability." Problems appeared on a computer screen, and participants were to respond as quickly and as accurately as they could. Steele and Aronson predicted that Black students would underperform on the test relative to White students if the test was relevant to the stereotype—that is, if it was diagnostic of their academic ability. On the other hand, Black students who took the very same test but under conditions in which the stereotype was less relevant would not show the underperformance effect. The results, presented in Fig. 5.1, reveal that this is precisely what happened. The statistical interaction between the race of the participants and the diagnosticity of the test was significant: Black students performed worse than any other group of students if, and only if, they thought the test was diagnostic. Black students performed well when they were assured that the test was not relevant to their academic ability.

Stereotype Threat and Gender

The stereotype is clear: Women are not as competent as men at technology, science, or math. They may be every bit the equal of men at the social

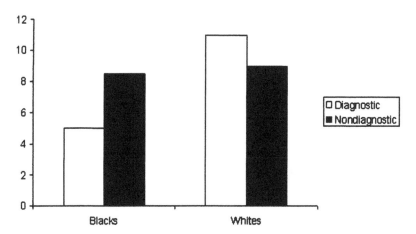

FIG. 5.1.   Test performance by race and diagnosticity of test (adapted from Steele & Aronson, 1995). Copyright © 1995 by the American Psychological Association. Adapted with permission.

sciences and even better at literature and the arts. But there is no doubt, according to the stereotype, that technology, science, and math are the province of men. Women performing any of these tasks, from programming computers to solving math problems to working at the laboratory bench, must face the "threat in the air"—the potential negative evaluation caused by the stereotype (Plaut, Cheryan, Rios, & Steele, 2003).

Spencer et al. (1999) had male and female students at the University of Michigan sit at a computer to take two math tests. Half of the men and half of the women were told that, in the past, one of the two tests had reliably shown gender differences but that the other had not. This explanation was designed to make it clear to the students that one of the tests was relevant to the gender stereotype but not the other test. It is interesting that Spencer et al. never explicitly told participants which way the gender differences "in the past" had come out, yet in interviews following the experiment, all students assumed that men had outperformed women.

The results were clear and dramatic. The test that was said to be relevant to the stereotype—that is, the one that had shown gender differences in the past—produced significant differences between the men and women. As we can see in the right-hand bars of Fig. 5.2, women responded to their computerized math test by performing worse than any of the groups. Men in the stereotype-relevant condition responded to the positive expectations by performing very well. Similarly, both men and women who had no reason to believe a test would be relevant to their gender category performed equally well. As in the Steele and Aronson (1995) study, people who are in a social category for which there is a negative stereotype perform poorly when that stereotype is made relevant to the task

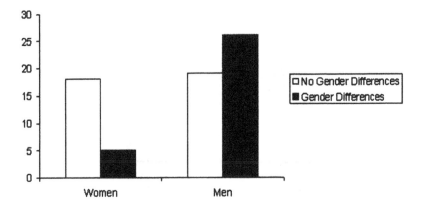

FIG. 5.2.   Test performance by gender depending on whether student was told test produced gender differences or not. Adapted from Spencer, S. J., Steele, C. M., & Quinn, D. M. (1999), Stereotype threat and women's math performance. *Journal of Experimental Social Psychology, 35,* 4–28, copyright © 1999, with permission from Elsevier.

at hand. In this study, the threat of confirming the stereotype undermined women's ability to show how well they could do at the math exam.

Identification With the Domain: How Much Do I Care?

Keeping a positive view of oneself as a capable and worthwhile person is one of life's basic and important motivations. In so many domains of life, people do what they can to protect their self-esteem from attack. We want to appear to others to be worthwhile and, perhaps most important, we want to believe that such an appraisal is true.

How we act forms a major part of our self-esteem. Our behaviors often reveal our values and our beliefs. Our generosity, helpfulness, and kindness are revealed through our behaviors. Our competencies are revealed through our performance. The woman who thinks of herself as an excellent golf player needs to shoot reasonably close to par; the tennis player needs to win some points on the court, and the honor student needs to score well on his or her exams. Negative stereotypes affect us because they threaten to undermine our competency in a particular domain. If we are sixth-grade students in a spelling contest but believe that children of our race, gender, or socioeconomic class do not do well at spelling, that stereotype arouses all of the concerns that we have been discussing. We will feel anxious and pressured to overcome the stereotype. But this only makes sense if we care about spelling—that is, if we feel invested in ourselves as spellers. Our self-esteem may rise and fall with our conception of ourselves as spelling bee winners and, if so, the threat posed by the stereotype is an awesome one. If we do not identify spelling as a domain that we care about, then our performance is less related to our feelings of self-worth. In such a case, our falling prey to the stereotype would make little difference.

Let's take an excursion away from academic pursuits and consider stereotype threat in the field of athletics. We probably all know people whose athletic skills are very important to them. They may play on organized teams or they may be weekend softball players, touch football players, or golfers. A missed pass, a bobbled play, or a successful putt may cause our athlete to spend the working or school week obsessing about her or his performance the last weekend. Their self-worth is very much intertwined with their athletic performance. On the other hand, there are many people for whom athletic events are much less important for their self-esteem. They may play occasionally, but they do not identify nearly as strongly with their sport. A stereotype that suggests to the former athlete that he or she may not do well because of their social category could be devastating to their sense of self-esteem. If they fail, if they confirm the stereotype, then their self-worth will be diminished. The latter athletes, on the other hand, will be less affected by the stereotype because their sense of self-esteem is not bound up with their athletic performance.

Empirically, we should find that people who are identified with a domain—that is, whose self-esteem is bound up with performance in that domain—will be the ones most likely to succumb to stereotype threat. And research results confirm this prediction. Pursuing the athletic domain, Jeff Stone and his colleagues (Stone, Lynch, Sjomeling, & Darley, 1999) asked White students at the University of Arizona to show their putting ability on a miniature golf course especially built for the laboratory. The students had taken a paper-and-pencil test that measured the degree of identification they had with sports. For example, students were asked to agree or disagree with such items as, "How I do athletically has little relation to who I really am." Stereotype threat was presented to some of the participants by convincing them that the test was a valid measure of "natural athletic ability." This is a dimension at which, according to the cultural stereotype, Black athletes are better than Whites. Stone et al. found that White students who felt that their athletic performance was part of their self-esteem were affected by the threat. It took them 28 putts to complete the miniature golf course. Golfers who received the stereotype threat but who did not couple their self-worth with their athletic performance took just 21 putts to complete the course. The threat created by the stereotype only affected those who identified themselves with golf, but did not affect the performance of disidentified golfers.

The same phenomenon holds true in academic pursuits. Let's return to the field of mathematics. Aronson and his colleagues (J. Aronson et al., 1999) invited students in an advanced calculus course at the University of

Texas to participate in a study in which they would take a general test of mathematics. The investigators administered a survey that measured the degree to which participants felt their sense self-esteem was invested in excelling at mathematics. They then had participants read a paragraph describing the stereotype. In this study, the threat was to White students' comparison with Asian Americans. In the threat condition, the paragraph made clear that Asian Americans usually outperform Whites on all measures of mathematics and that the current test was going to be used to make national comparisons of math ability by race. Aronson et al. found that the threat caused by the stereotype of White inferiority to Asians affected only those students for whom mathematics was an integral part of their self-esteem. When there was no threat, or when there was a threat to students who did not care about mathematics, performance on the test was high. However, the students who performed most poorly on the math exam were those who cared about mathematics and who were subjected to the stereotype threat. In short, identification with the domain being tested is crucial for stereotype threat to cause a reduction in performance.

Identification With My Group: How Much Do I Care?

People can identify with a performance domain and be devastated by the potential negative stereotype that applies to their group. When the groups are social categories, membership in the group is automatic. An African American student is a member of his or her group by reason of genetics. A woman is in her social group because of her chromosomal combination. Stereotypes that apply to her group affect her because, in most cases, she is undeniably a member of that group. However, in chapter 2 we noted that computer anxiety affects girls not solely as a function of biological sex but more importantly as a function of how much they identify with their psychological gender. In the research by Brosnan (1998), we showed that although membership in the social category *female* was dichotomous, the degree of identification with femininity determined the degree of computer anxiety for the girls in the study.

Toni Schmader (2002) examined a similar question with stereotype threat. She asked male and female students at the University of Arizona, all of whom had high SAT scores in math, to take a newly devised test of mathematics ability. In the condition designed to invoke the negative stereotype of women's mathematics ability, the experimenter indicated that he was interested in using the new test to compare women's and men's mathematical scores and that he would be using each person's score as an indicator of women's or men's math ability in general. In the condition designed to minimize stereotype threat, the experimenter merely indicated that the scores would be used to assess each individual's mathematics ability. No mention of gender was made. In addition, in the "no threat" condition, participants merely put their initials on the front page of the exam. In the "threat" condition, they indicated their sex.

Schmader's research differed from prior studies because she also asked participants to fill out a scale designed to measure how much they identified with their gender. Items included, "Being a woman/man is an important part of my self-image" and "Being a woman/man is unimportant to my sense of what kind of person I am." By summing the items on the scale, Schmader identified a group of men and women for whom gender was highly relevant and a group for whom it was not relevant. For students taking the exam who were not threatened by the stereotype, gender identification made no difference. All of the students scored well on the test. However, look at the data in Fig. 5.3 that shows test performance for students who were under stereotype threat. Women who did not feel that being female was particularly important for their self-identity performed almost identically as men the men who did not feel that masculinity was important. However, on the right side of the graph, we see the enormous difference that stereotype threat made to men and women of high ability. Men were buoyed by the positive expectation for their gender and did very well. Highly gender-identified women, despite their equally high SAT scores, performed more poorly on the test than any other group in the experiment. It is the psychological identification with gender, combined with the negative stereotype, that produced the deleterious impact on performance.

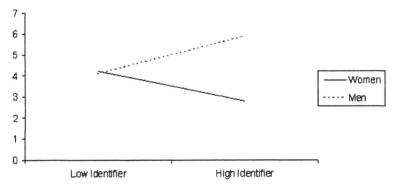

FIG. 5.3.   Number correct as a function of gender and degree to which test takers identify with gender. Reprinted from Schmader, T. (2002), Gender identification moderates stereotype threat effects on women's math performance. *Journal of Experimental Social Psychology, 38,* 194–201, copyright © 2002, with permission from Elsevier.

What Causes the Damage?

In Steele's view, the damage of stereotype threat is caused by pressure and anxiety. People fear that they will be viewed as part of a negative stereotype. Although the stereotype is always present, it only works on people's minds when the performance bears on the stereotype and it is made salient that they are members of the group that has a negative expectation. It also only works when people feel identified with the domain in question. In those instances, people feel that others will see them only through the lens of the stereotype. They feel pressure to show that they are not like the stereotype and live in constant fear that they will do something to confirm the stereotype. The woman sitting at her computer, for example, fears making the error that will show her peers that, just as expected, she is not competent with computers.

If this is true, then people's anxiety should mediate the effect of stereotype threat. That is, if people are asked about their level of anxiety when performing a task, stereotype threat should cause high levels of anxiety and the higher the level of anxiety, the more likely should be the reduction of the level of performance. And other things should happen as well. People under high stereotype threat may be highly distracted, thinking about the stereotype rather than the task. They may also worry about what other people are thinking and how their own performance will be viewed by others.

One study presents convincing evidence for the role played by anxiety and evaluation worry in producing the deleterious effects of stereotype threat. In the study we discussed earlier in which women at the University of Michigan were placed under stereotype threat while doing mathematics problems (Spencer et al., 1999), participants filled out measures of their levels of anxiety and the degree to which they worried about other people's evaluations of them. Both of these measures were significant mediators of test performance. The higher the stereotype threat, the higher the anxiety and worry about evaluation. And the higher the anxiety and evaluation worry, the lower were the scores on the math exam. At least in this stereotype threat study on perception of mathematics abilities, the increase in anxiety and increase in evaluation worry were responsible for the reduced performance.

THE CASE OF MULTIPLE IDENTITIES

Each of us has more than one social identity. Jared, for example, is in the social category *boy*. He may also be White and come from a medium-size city. His grandparents immigrated to the United States from Portugal. Immediately, he carries identities from the social categories *urban, Portu-*

guese, and *White.* He may also be identified with his Little League team, his elementary school, and his gymnastic club. Martha, too, has multiple identities that characterize her social categories. She has social identities from being *female, suburban, White, Swedish,* and a member of her soccer team. If Martha primarily thinks of herself as Swedish when she is in computer or math class, then the negative stereotype that applies to females at these subjects may not weigh on her mind. If she thinks of herself primarily as a girl, then she is vulnerable to the effects of stereotype threat. Similarly, if Jared thinks of himself as a boy, he may be prepared to do very well on his IT assignments. But if he thinks of himself as White, then stereotype threat may affect his performance on the basketball team (Stone, Perry, & Darley, 1997).

Stereotype threat occurs when a particularly vulnerable social identity is made accessible to people. We say that a category is *accessible* when it is the one that is most likely to come to mind—that is, when it is, so to speak, on the top of the list of possible identities and thus most likely to be chosen when people think of their social groups. People know that they are in a variety of groups and categories. But there are often factors in the situation that make one identity more accessible than another. For example, if a teacher were to tell you that a test you are taking is useful in comparing abilities by race, then your identity as Black, White, or Asian may become particularly accessible. It is not that you forget that you are also male or female, but gender becomes less accessible at that moment than race. Conversely, if a researcher tells you that a test is comparing the math abilities of males vs. females, then your gender identity rises to the top, and your racial identity becomes less accessible. Whether you will be affected by a negative stereotype of your group depends, in large part, on whether your social identity as a member of that group is made salient.

A very interesting study that examined multiple social identities was reported by Shih, Pittinsky, and Ambady (1999). The participants in their study were Asian American women at a prestigious university in the United States. The students' task was to take a difficult test of their mathematics abilities. As we know, there is a pervasive negative stereotype for women's abilities in mathematics and several studies have shown its deleterious effects on women's performance in math (J. Aronson et al., 1999; Schmader, 2003; Spencer et al., 1999). But Shih and her colleagues reasoned that there is a positive stereotype of Asian Americans' ability to perform particularly well in math and technology. If the women thought of themselves as primarily Asian American, then they would not be affected by the negative stereotype for females but rather would be buoyed by the positive racial stereotype that applies to Asian Americans' mathematics abilities.

Prior to taking the test, all participants were given a questionnaire to fill out about themselves. The questions they were asked were designed to make one of their multiple identities salient and accessible. In the female-identity condition, the students were asked seemingly innocuous questions about their campus life. The questions caused the students to think of their identity as women. For example, students were asked whether their dormitories were single-sex or co-ed. They were asked to list three reasons why they would prefer a single-sex floor in their dormitory, then were asked for three reasons why they would prefer a co-ed floor. These questions did not overtly tell the participants to think of themselves as women, but they certainly made being female rise to the top of the various social identities these students possessed.

Another group of the Asian American women were asked questions that brought Asian-identity to the top of the list. They were asked about the languages they spoke at home, whether they had an opportunity to speak these languages in their residence halls, and how many generations of their family had lived in America. A third group was a control group in which neither of the identities was made salient. These students were given a questionnaire that asked about university telephone, television, and communication services.

Shih et al. (1999) predicted that the threat of a negative stereotype would hurt the performance of the Asian American women who were primed to have their female identities most accessible. Conversely, they predicted that the group that was induced to think about their Asian roots would respond to the positive stereotype and perform better than women in the control group for whom neither identity was made salient. The results confirmed the predictions. As we can see in Fig. 5.4, women in the

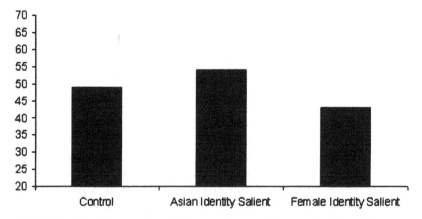

FIG. 5.4. Percentage of math items answered correctly depending on which social identity is made salient (adapted from Shih et al., 1999).

control condition answered 49% of the math items correctly. Women whose Asian American identity had been made salient improved to 54% correct, whereas women whose female identification had been made salient fell to 43%.

From these results, we can see that making an identity salient can have positive or negative effects on performance, depending on the stereotype that applies to that identity. In an interesting extension of these results, Shih et al. (1999) conducted a second study, again involving Asian women as the participants. This time, the study, using the same procedure, was conducted in Vancouver, Canada. Shih et al. suggested that the stereotype of Asians in western Canada is very different from the stereotype in most of the United States. In Vancouver, the Asian community is more recently immigrated. Because Asian immigration to Vancouver is very recent, the stereotype is more working class and less intellectual. Therefore, priming either the female identity or the Asian identity should allow the stereotype threat to affect performance. Indeed, whereas Asian Canadian women in a control group answered 59% of the math items correctly, that number dropped to 44% for women whose Asian identity was primed and to 28% for the women whose gender was primed. It is the combination of a person's accessible social identity with the valence of the stereotype for that group that determines whether stereotype threat affects performance.

Making Identities Salient: The Double-Edged Sword of Tokenism

The research in stereotype threat has shown a variety of ways to make a person's identity salient. People can be asked to write down their race or gender, they can answer questions that more subtly bring gender or racial issues to the forefront of their thinking, they can be told that the task is especially relevant to gender or racial issues. There is yet another way to make people's identity salient that forces them to confront a negative stereotype of their group. When people are a distinct minority in their group settings, that status automatically brings their social identity to the fore. For example, minority-group school children spontaneously mention their ethnicity more when they are merely asked to describe themselves (McGuire & McGuire, 1981).

Consider the situation of a Black student who perseveres in his urban environment, attains good grades, and advances to college. There, he finds himself to be one of the few Blacks at his college. This racial minority status brings racial identity to the foreground. Without anyone needing to mention his race, without special priming manipulations that characterized the experiments we have just described, this student's social identity as an African American will be salient and accessible. Knowing the negative stereotype that is applied to his group, all of the conditions for stereotype threat are present. He will not only have to learn what his instructor is teaching him, he will constantly have to battle that "threat in the air."

A schoolgirl is interested in science and technology. She eagerly does her math and science homework every night, and sees herself as a budding scientist or engineer. In high school, she enrolls in the difficult algebra courses and notices that there are more boys than girls in the class. As a sophomore, she takes advance trigonometry and finds that the number of girls has dwindled still farther. By the time she enrolls in calculus and advanced computer science, she is the solo or "token" female in her class. We use the term *token* to refer to extreme minority status within a group (Lord & Saenz, 1985), even though she may not be the *only* member of her gender in the class. Remember the girls we described in chapter 2 who were enrolled in the advanced computer science classes at Whitfield High School in suburban Pittsburgh. These few girls were tokens, the very few who had enrolled in the class, and they were constantly aware of their social identity as females.

Not only is the token status likely to raise the stereotype threat problem whose deleterious effects we have seen in considerable recent research, tokenism may have problems that transcend, or add to, stereotype threat. Tokens are constantly aware of their "outsider's" role in an otherwise homogeneous group. She constantly must negotiate her public identity, knowing that she is representing her group in front of the others. She knows that how she acts, what she says, and how well she performs are all matters of particular scrutiny. In short, everyone else in the group is watching *her*. She is not one of many, but rather she is in the spotlight. Everything she does matters because everything will be noticed. Moreover, she is the representative of her social category in the larger social group. How she is perceived may reflect on all members of her group. Worrying that you are in the spotlight, worrying about how people perceive you, and worrying about how you reflect on your social category all require cognitive resources. They demand attention. And we know that when attention is divided, people cannot perform any of their tasks very well.

The conclusion this leads to is that anyone in the position of a token—a member of a minority within an otherwise homogeneous majority—will perform less well at the group's task. Too many resources are devoted to worrying about self-presentation and representing one's group for there to be a full set of resources remaining for the task at hand. Lord and Saenz (1985) tested this prediction in the laboratory. College students volunteered for a study on group interaction. Their task was to discuss their opinions on a variety of topics with three other college students. The participant either found that there were two men and two women in the group, or that the three other group members were of the opposite sex. They knew that, at the end of the discussion, they would be asked questions that assessed their memory for what the other group members had said.

Token minorities are typically worried that they are being carefully scrutinized by other group members, and they are undoubtedly correct in this fear. Observers to the group interaction remembered everything the token said better than they remembered what members of the majority said. The token minority members were indeed in the spotlight and what they said was perceived and remembered. Unfortunately, tokens did not fare well when asked what they remembered about the interactions. When asked how many of the opinions they remembered, token group members recalled only 35% of the opinions expressed in the group. Nontoken members remembered nearly 50%.

Note that this performance decrement had nothing to do with stereotype threat. It happened for males as well as females, with no difference between the genders. If someone had solo status because of gender, that person remembered the conversation more poorly than if he or she was not a solo token. Simply being a token minority caused the recall deficit.

Let us recall Denise, a student in Janet Schofield's (1995) study at Whitmore High School. She had persevered through her mathematics and science courses to be able to take a high school class in computer science. The more highly identified she felt toward courses in IT, the more she wanted to be in the courses. However, each year, Denise became more of a minority due to gender. By the time she reached the advanced IT class, she was one of but a handful of girls who continued their studies in information technology. Her identification with IT caused her to continue, but that very same identification made her more and more of a token female. And tokenism made it all the more difficult for her to succeed. In addition to the comments she received from her peers and the attitudes of her teacher (see chapter 2), Denise was subjected to the effects caused by tokenism per se. Like the students in Lord and Saenz's (1985) study, Denise's attention to her work was undoubtedly divided by her apprehension of being the representative of the category *girls* in computer science. Her work was likely to suffer as a consequence. Moreover, because others in the class pay more attention to the minority token than they do to majority members of the group, any mistakes Denise may have made did not escape her classmates' and her teacher's attention. Add stereotype threat to the effects of tokenism and we have a true double-dip dilemma. In order for Denise to succeed, she must overcome the effects of stereotype threat and tokenism, just to be able to perform to the best of her ability. The irony of the double-edged sword is that the more Denise really cares about computer science, the more exposed she is to becoming a token and to suffering the effects of stereotype threat. Do some women make it? Certainly, they do. But the road is so difficult that it is not surprising that more women drop out than succeed.

FURTHER CONSEQUENCES OF STEREOTYPE THREAT: DISIDENTIFICATION

The pressure to disconfirm a social stereotype occurs when people care about the domain that is being tested. When the White golfer cared about his athletic identity, he succumbed to stereotype threat (Stone et al., 1999). When the students cared about their mathematical abilities, the negative stereotype caused them to perform worse on a test (J. Aronson et al., 1999). The basic motivation for feeling the extra pressure of the negative stereotype comes from the basic human desire to achieve and keep a high sense of self-esteem. Any threat to one's standing on that important domain is a threat to self-esteem.

One way to deal with threats to self-esteem is to *disidentify* with the domain in question. If a person no longer feels that her self-esteem is bound up with her academic performance, then a poor report card may be a blow to her parents, but it will not reduce the student's feeling of self-worth. One invidious effect of suffering the anxiety of stereotype threat is to run from it. By disidentifying with the domain in question, it can no longer affect you.

Denise, our high school student in chapter 3, has persisted with her computer education despite the derision by her peers and the insensitivity of her teachers. She continues to feel that IT education is important to her and she continues to identify with the domain. But other students who were once as committed as Denise may have decided that the threat to their self-esteem was too severe. In the face of forces that include stereotype threat, tokenism, unhealthy attributions made about their abilities, they may well decide to disidentify with the computer domain. "It's not worth it," they may feel. Rather than persevering with computer education, they may remove it as part of their self-concept, choosing instead more stereotype-consistent pursuits.

All is not lost, however. Despite the pessimism and the uphill nature of the battle, there are ways to overcome the effects of stereotype threat and the other factors we have been discussing. In the next two chapters, we consider some of the suggestions to remediate the impact of these social forces. Some of our suggestions are specific to the problems encountered by girls as they make their way through the educational system. Others, like suggestions to remediate stereotype threat, are broad and include some of the more general phenomena to which stereotype threat applies. Some are based on published empirical evidence (Cohen, Steele, & Ross, 1999), while other suggestions are presented as potential solutions to the problems that empirical research has identified.

CHAPTER

6

Working Toward Solutions

We began our discussion of the gender-based digital divide by focusing on Jared and Martha, two young children ready to begin a lifelong journey through the educational process. If they are typical children, they will each learn a great deal as they proceed through school, and they will each become prepared to take their place in society. However, the likelihood that Martha will be as prepared as Jared to find opportunities in technological fields is not high. The likelihood that she will profit from educational experiences that require the use of computers is not equal to Jared's. The likelihood that Martha will be as prepared as Jared for the technologically oriented careers of the 21st century is lower than it should be.

Must it be so? We think not. Although there are no easy solutions to complex societal problems, our analyses thus far lead us to believe that some solutions are possible. Just as there is no specific sector to blame for the current problem, there is no single entity responsible for fixing it. Although often unconsciously, parents, peers and educators have all contributed to sustaining the digital divide. Parents have provided boys and girls with their early views of themselves—their strengths, their weaknesses—as well as having shaped their views of what activities are appropriate to engage in. Parents not only communicate their own values and aspirations as they raise their children, but they also communicate the values of society at large. Children also learn from each other. Especially when they enter school, peers help to communicate society's attitudes to each other. If those attitudes include a view that computers are the province of boys, then peers can and do persistently reinforce those notions.

The formal educational system reinforces society's attitudes as well. Teachers, as particularly influential adults, may unwittingly communicate society's values about girls' ability in science, math, and technology to their students. Moreover, the very structure of classroom activities can multiply the problem by placing computer use in contexts that are public and competitive. The educational system chooses the software that will guide children's journey into the realm of technology. The frequent choice of male-oriented, competitive software continues to foster the digital divide.

In this chapter, we return to our discussion of developmental, contextual, and psychological factors to offer suggestions for overcoming the digital divide. Some suggestions are apparent; others are more subtle. Some require a great deal of effort and funding, but others require only awareness and the desire for change. We think that the primary impediment for change is the lack of awareness of the problem and the ways in which we all contribute to it. Armed with greater awareness, wise decision making by parents and educators can address the causes of computer anxiety, disidentification with computers, negative expectations, and inappropriate attributions at their roots. This chapter is dedicated to that goal.

A MODEL FOR UNDERSTANDING THE DIGITAL DIVIDE

In Figs. 6.1 and 6.2, we outline a model depicting the key processes we think contribute to the digital divide. Although we think that the model has much heuristic value as a road map organizing many of the important factors currently contributing to the digital divide, our intention here is not to provide an exhaustive list of all factors. We have represented important links between factors and concepts with arrows. In our model, we have focused our attention on the links that have been widely studied and are most relevant to our discussion. Additional research is needed to uncover other important linkages between some of the other concepts and to elaborate on the links that we have specified here.

At the heart of the digital divide is the individual student. She is the one experiencing computer anxiety, forming negative attitudes toward the computer, developing expectations for her performance, and, in certain contexts, performing more poorly on computer tasks. In the end, she is also the one who decides why she did not perform well on those tasks. Figures 6.1 and 6.2 depict some of the key processes that are located within the individual student as well as the outside forces that influence those processes. The student must cope with her own level of computer anxiety, the attributions she makes about her level of ability and the degree of identification she experiences with computers. Anything that increases her computer anxiety, leads her to doubt her ability, or causes her to disidentify with computers will lead her to form negative attitudes about computers and technology.

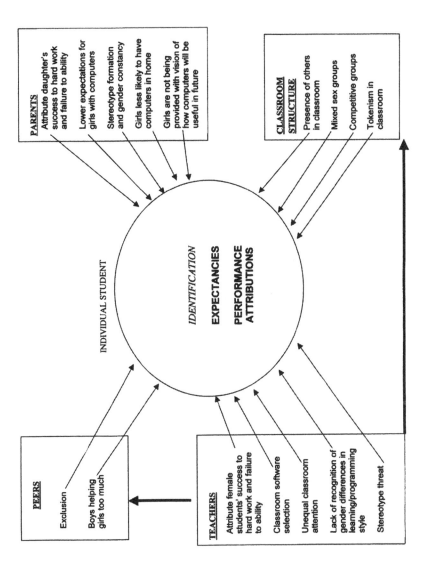

FIG. 6.1. Influences acting on individual student.

PARENTS
- Attribute daughter's success to hard work and failure to ability
- Lower expectations for girls with computers
- Stereotype formation and gender constancy
- Girls less likely to have computers in home
- Girls are not being provided with vision of how computers will be useful in future

CLASSROOM STRUCTURE
- Presence of others in classroom
- Mixed sex groups
- Competitive groups
- Tokenism in classroom

INDIVIDUAL STUDENT

IDENTIFICATION

EXPECTANCIES

PERFORMANCE ATTRIBUTIONS

PEERS
- Exclusion
- Boys helping girls too much

TEACHERS
- Attribute female students' success to hard work and failure to ability
- Classroom software selection
- Unequal classroom attention
- Lack of recognition of gender differences in learning/programming style
- Stereotype threat

INDIVIDUAL STUDENT

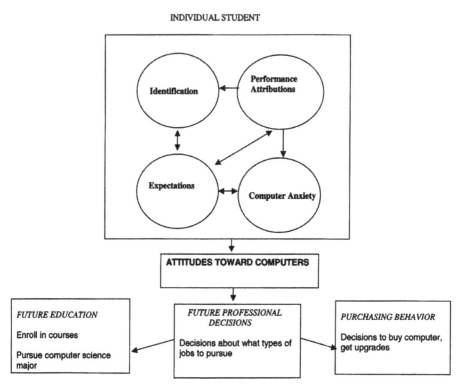

FIG. 6.2.   Model of individual student.

Negative attitudes, in turn, will mean that she is more likely to avoid lessons, classes, and careers involving computers. Of course, anxiety, expectations, disidentification, and attributions are not independent and are related to each other in many ways. For instance, young women who do not identify with computers (i.e, feel that computers are not for people like them) may, in turn, feel more anxious when using computers. Young women who experience computer anxiety may also attribute any evidence of failure to their inability to understand technology. Nonetheless, it is useful to think of these processes operating within the individual as somewhat distinct, with each contributing to the digital divide in very direct ways.

As the model shows, the intra-individual variables are primarily affected by important influences in the social environment. For convenience, Fig. 6.1 divides these influences as those coming primarily from the educational system, and those coming from parents and peers. We further divide the educational system into factors that are centered directly in the interpersonal contact between student and teacher and those that come from more structural elements of the school and classroom.

Parents

Parents are the primary socializing agents. From the first moments of life, parents represent the point of contact with the world. As children grow, parents select the toys, the books, and the entertainment to which the children are exposed. Children also learn much about themselves from the reactions of their parents. Are they cute? Are they smart? Do they like to read and write? The socialization goes on every day, much of it without deliberate thought. We begin by taking a look at some of the actions parents can take, even when their children are very young, to encourage girls to take their place in the technological revolution.

Learning What Is Appropriate for Your Gender. As we saw in chapter 2, children's concept of what it means to be a boy or a girl is rather fluid. Young girls believe that they can be boys if they dress like boys; young boys believe they can be girls if they dress like girls. The notion that gender is constant becomes clear to children near the age of 7. At this stage of development, children also learn to incorporate the social meaning of gender. They learn the attitudes and behaviors that accompany being a boy or girl. It is not too much of a caricature to say that boys learn that playing with trucks is in their domain. Playing with Barbie dolls is in the girls' domain.

Parents must be vigilant to disabuse children of unwanted gender stereotypes, especially near the age of gender constancy. Remember that stereotypes about what is appropriate for girls and boys can be quite subtle. They come from stories that we choose to read to our children, portrayals on television, and information provided by peers in school and in the backyard. Because parents are in an especially influential role, they can disabuse the stereotypes. They can make it clear to children that all types of choices are open to both boys and girls. Girls can and should do well at computers, mathematics, and science. If this message is instilled prior to the age of gender constancy, we will have a better chance to overcome the digital divide. Being attentive to the stereotype, the timing, and the remedy is a suggestion for all parents.

Encouraging Positive Attributions and Expectations. Parents have been called the "expectancy socializers" (Parsons et al., 1982). As children grow and take on more tasks, parents form their own attitudes about their children's abilities. In chapter 4, we saw that parents' attitudes and expectations about their children's performance affected the children's expectations as well. If parents believe that girls simply do not have the ability to tackle computer tasks, then the girls will take on the same attitude. They will expect to fail. If girls do well at a task for which their parents believe they have limited ability, such as technology, then parents are likely to attribute the success to luck or to the possibility that it was merely an easy version of the task. If girls do not succeed at a computer task, parents attribute that failure to a lack of ability. More important, girls adopt the same set of attributions for themselves. Even a minor failure at a computer task, such as a momentary misunderstanding of the instructions, can lead girls to confirm their lack of ability. On the other hand, they credit luck for their success.

Once again, parental vigilance and awareness can ameliorate this problem. We must educate parents to understand that they, too, fall prey to the nefarious effects of society's stereotypes. All children need to be encouraged to see their successes at IT as testimony to their ability rather than to luck. It is certainly true that not all children can achieve unlimited heights on the computer, and it is important for children to have realistic assessments of their abilities. It is even more important, though, not to limit children's quest for achievement just because the children are girls learning or working at a gender stereotypic task such as IT. Parents must convince themselves that girls have every bit the same ability at IT as boys and they must reinforce that attitude in their children.

Make Computers Available to Daughters as Well as Sons; Encourage Their Use.   Surveys show that parents are more likely to purchase computers for their sons than for their daughters. When they purchase computers, they spend more money on technology for boys than they do for girls. Girls report that they are less likely to have computers and that they are less likely than boys to be encouraged to use them.

Parents must become as enthusiastic about encouraging their daughters to use computers as they are for their sons. We suspect that when girls use computers at home, parents think of it as cute. If they are not interested in computers, then so be it. However, when boys use computers at home, parents think of it as necessary. A lack of interest by boys in the family's PC or Mac is a disaster. It is necessary to remember that girls and boys have equal need to be comfortable on the computer. Whether it is playing a game, researching material, writing e-mail or doing homework, girls need to be encouraged to spend time on the family's computer. If the family does not have a computer for economic reasons, many schools and libraries have loaner programs or at least make computers available at their facilities.

Whenever possible, it is also important for boys and girls to see that adult women use the computer as well as adult men. Simply put, moms should spend time on the computer so that sons and daughters view technology as something that adults make use of rather than just dads. This will help boys and girls resist the idea that technology is gender linked—that is, that it is a toy or tool primarily for men.

Another value of encouraging computer use at home is that it can provide a non-threatening context for teaching girls that making errors on the computer is acceptable. Teachers have noted that girls seem afraid that they will break the machine if they hit the wrong key; boys seem to have no such worries. Indeed, in Robinson-Stavely and Cooper's (1990) study with college students, women were far less likely to just *try* something when they needed to solve a problem. Men, on the other hand, made numerous attempts to find the solutions by simply trying many actions. Even though the majority of their attempts led nowhere, the mere willingness to try various solutions eventually produced success. Parents and teachers can encourage girls not to fear making mistakes on the computer. Such lessons may be more successful at home because of the less threatening environment that the home usually provides. Showing girls that the computer will not break because they tried incorrect key strokes, and that they have a greater chance to succeed at their task, will be a major help to girls as they proceed through school and into adulthood.

Consider Forming Voluntary Girls-Only Clubs. What kinds of experiences can make girls feel comfortable with technology? Voluntary after-school programs and summer camps can provide wonderful experiences to enhance children's comfort with computers. However, these well-intentioned activities may have the ironic consequence of undermining girls' confidence while enhancing only the boys'. We have seen that girls "vote with their feet," showing how they feel about technology by staying away in droves from voluntary mixed-gender computer activities. The girls who do attend have to be strong enough to overcome several built-in traps that can make their experience less than positive. Not only may girls suffer from many of the social forces that tilt the playing field against them in the regular classroom, but in clubs and camps, the problem may be still worse. For example, anxiety due to the social context of computing, the nature of the software, and the effects of social stereotypes do not disappear merely because girls are participating with technology in extracurricular situations. And, because camps and clubs have very few females who attend, it is likely that the girls who do sign up for such activities will feel even more like token representatives of their gender, thus increasing their marginalization and stigmatization. It may also exacerbate the tendency for instructors to rely on male-oriented software and male-oriented examples. After all, the boys will so heavily outnumber the girls, that it may seem all the more natural to select material that intrigues boys rather than interests the few girls in the group.

Parents should seriously consider forming, or having their daughters join, computer clubs designed for exclusively for girls. Lichtman (1998) described a very successful girls-only computer club in Allentown, Pennsylvania. The Cyber Sisters Club opened its doors to 15 fifth-grade girls in the spring of 1998. Activities were based on the premise that girls will buy into technology primarily when they see how it relates to their own interests and preferences (Brunner, 1997; Furger, 1998). Cyber Sisters focused on social activities such as chat rooms and e-mail. It taught girls to find information on the Internet for special topics of interest, such as learning about the BackStreet Boys, the Spice Girls, Leonardo DiCaprio, and all-time favorites like Winnie the Pooh. Girls also learned how to create their own personal web pages and they "shopped" for graphics designs to beautify them.

The 15 girls from Allentown, who had had only limited experience with computers prior to attending the Cyber Sisters Club, became highly enthusiastic and accomplished at using the computer. Lichtman cites the nonthreatening atmosphere that was facilitated by not having to compete with boys and by teachers' attitudes that were pointedly encouraging and enthusiastic. In addition, the ability to use their time to focus on activities and examples that were consistent with girls' interests made the experience a relevant and rewarding one for girls. As we said earlier in this book, computers in typical classrooms often function like communications designed for boys. In the Cyber Sisters Club, the communication was very directly related to girls, and they responded with enjoyment and enthusiasm.

Smith College, one of the premier women's colleges in the United States, offers a summer program exclusively for girls. Its official Web site sets its mission in the following terms: "Girls can grow up to be great scientists. Many have. And yet, nearly a century after Marie Curie became the first person to win two Nobel Prizes, bright, ambitious high-school girls are often skeptical of their scientific abilities." One of its 2001 campers commented at the end of the summer, "I've learned that being a girl and loving science is totally ok."

Parents should advocate for the creation of girls-only computer clubs and summer camps. In the following chapter, we consider seriously the benefits and drawbacks of girls-only classes for technology and girls-only schools. In this section, however, we suggest that voluntary participation in clubs that are designed exclusively for girls can have productive and measurable benefits for girls. Schools will probably be cooperative with helping to create such experiences if parents request them. So, too, will other civic groups, such as local YMCA/YWCA or community organizations. Giving girls the opportunity to learn in a way that makes them comfortable will allow them to see the benefits of technology for pursuing their own interests and exploring their own values. Once armed with sufficient skill, competence, and confidence, girls will be in a far better position to participate as equals in the computer experiences provided in their regular local schools. They may also gain the confidence and skill to participate more fully in the technological revolution that will characterize the rewarding careers of the 21st century.

The Classroom Teacher

What can teachers do to help overcome the digital divide? Teachers are typically the first major influence on youngsters after the family itself. Whether it is pre-school, nursery school, or kindergarten, teachers become the first consistent representative of the social world beyond home. Their influence on the development of the child is enormous.

Teachers will play an essential role in any program designed to dispel the digital divide. Teachers can help to rectify mistaken ideas that children bring with them to school that may have been communicated by parents and peers. Teachers can carefully structure their classrooms in ways that minimize the negative effects of peers on girls' identification with computers. Teachers can also monitor their own behavior so that they neither cause nor exacerbate the reluctance that girls have about technology. Any adverse influence that a teacher may have on girls' conceptions of their ability and interest in pursuing computers and information technology is surely unintentional. Becoming aware of how they may be contributing to the digital divide and steps they may take to alleviate the problem will help teachers contribute to the solution.

Choose the Software Wisely. School systems pour an enormous amount of money into their technology programs. Much of the funding and the attention is devoted to hardware and operating systems. Should they purchase a mainframe? Should they purchase MacIntosh or DOS system machines? Should they support UNIX? How shall they connect to the Internet? Shall there be computer classrooms, or shall every classroom have computers? Far less attention is spent on software. What tasks will children actually perform on the computer? What manufacturers produce good software programs? Will children actually learn something from those programs? If they don't learn much, will they at least enjoy it? In many schools, teachers and principals are on their own when it comes to the daunting task of finding appropriate material to put on the computer.

In this book, we have documented the negative impact that inappropriate software can have on children. Many of the computer programs designed for young children contain the formal features that appeal to boys: competitive activities and story lines containing sports, space, or war. Girls are invited to learn from this software, but they certainly do not feel welcome.

Teachers must be especially vigilant to avoid any IT programs that rely on the factors that only boys prefer. Exploding missiles, the hitting of homeruns, and scoring of touchdowns may look appealing. They may come with sounds and lights that make us assume that they are motivating for children. As we have seen, however, these programs motivate boys, not girls. Avoiding such software is not an easy task for two reasons. One is that such software is prevalent in the educational market. A second reason is that, unless we are extremely vigilant, we have a tendency to assume that computer software is appropriate when it is male-oriented. Recall the study by Huff and Cooper (1987) that we described in chapter 4. In that research, teachers eagerly wrote computer programs that were replete with male metaphors when they imagined that they were writing for students in general. Our automatic assumption that computers communicate with boys makes us vulnerable to missing the inappropriateness of the IT software for teaching girls.

What should appropriate software look like? This is not an easy question to answer, but we would like to raise an important issue. One suggestion is to create software that girls would enjoy, using some of the stories and characters that girls find appealing, and to have such software available in classrooms at all levels. Indeed, a mathematics program for girls might feature a digitized Barbie who needs to figure out the correct dimensions for making a dress. This would immerse Barbie and the student into solving geometric and algebraic problems. Boys, on the other hand, could learn similar skills from an adventure in which their space ship traverses the planets of outer space. However, with this solution, we risk solving one problem by exacerbating another one. One value that marks modern education is an effort to eradicate inappropriate and unnecessary gender distinctions. Encouraging girls to identify with a gender-stereotypic character and permitting boys to continue to identify with aggressive adventures may permit both genders to perform well with computers. However, it will also reify the general social stereotypes about what is appropriate for girls and boys.

A second solution, and one that we endorse, is to search for gender-neutral software. Gender-neutral software would de-emphasize gender stereotypes of both kinds. Learning would not take place as a way to solve an intergalactic fight nor would it help Barbie create the latest fashion. Instead, it would be based on activities that are interesting to both sexes and are relevant to the educational task at hand. There are several good examples of such programs that have been successful in classrooms in recent years. We recommend that teachers be especially vigilant to find educationally appropriate, gender-neutral software for all phases of their classroom activities.

Provide Equal Access to Computers.   Computers should be equally available to all students in a classroom. We doubt that teachers would ever intentionally create a situation in which boys have preferential access to computers. Nonetheless, in the real world of the classroom, it may often turn out that way. In the younger grades, computers are often available as optional activities. Teachers have commented that boys are the ones who more often choose to play their favorite games on the computer. Girls choose an alternate activity, or watch the boys play their computer games. Although this is technically equal access, in reality it is not. Boys gravitate to the computers either because the software appeals to them or because of attitudes toward computers they have learned at home. Girls are not enamored by the software and may have entered school with more negative attitudes, possibly based on the stereotypes they learned at home. Choosing not to play with the computer when it is available adds to girls' self-conception that computers are not for them. We recommend that computers be used equally by all children. Every child, boy and girl, should have time scheduled for working with IT programs on the computer either in regular classrooms or in specially designated computer classrooms.

Attend to Boys and Girls ... Equally.   Imagine Jared and Martha in their elementary school class. Each of them is attempting to learn how to master an exercise on the computer. When they have questions, will the teacher respond to Jared and Martha in the same way? Will the teacher call on each of them equally often? How will their work be evaluated? Most teachers believe that they treat boys and girls equally in their classrooms. Yet, research has shown that teachers unwittingly but systematically treat boys and girls differently.

In *A Guide to Gender Fair Education in Science and Mathematics,* Burger and Sandy (1998) report a few disturbing observations. When teaching science and math, teachers inadvertently initiate more interactions with boys than with girls, they call on boys more frequently than they call on girls, praise boys for the *content* of their work but praise girls for the *appearance* of their work. Teachers respond differently to boys' and girls' requests for help. They are more apt to encourage boys to obtain answers for themselves while they tend to give girls the answers directly. In general, boys demand and receive more attention than girls. It is not surprising that girls emerge from such treatment with a lowered sense of efficacy, and less confidence in their ability to solve problems in information technology.

Burger and Sandy (1998) suggest that teachers carefully monitor their own behavior to make certain that they are treating girls with behaviors that imply the same respect for their abilities and accomplishments that they convey to boys. They suggest that teachers ask themselves very systematic questions about their expectations and actions. Several checklists have been developed to help teachers monitor their own behavior as they deliver instruction in technology, science, and mathematics (Grayson & Martin, 1988; Sadker & Sadker, 1994; Virginia Space Grant Consortium, 1996). For example, the Virginia Consortium checklist asks teachers to rate themselves on such items as, "I do not refer to all doctors as 'he' or nurses and secretaries as 'she.'" Campbell and Storo (1994) suggest that teachers can supplement their own self-evaluations by asking peers or students to collect some hard data about their behavior in the classroom. Either a fellow teacher or a student can count the number of boys and girls the teacher calls on, and can evaluate whether boys or girls are asked similar questions—for example, who is asked specific questions of fact and who is asked more complex interpretative questions. Because gender bias in the classroom is almost always inadvertent, using self-rating scales and examining the objective observations of others can help teachers respond with equal encouragement, enthusiasm, and expectations to the boys and girls in their classrooms.

Reducing the Problem of Stereotype Threat.   Girls understand the stereotype that affects them: Computers are the province of boys, not girls. Girls are not supposed to enjoy working or playing with computers; they traditionally do less well at technology than boys. The forces acting on children, ranging from the attitudes of parents to the expectations of software manufacturers, have contributed to this belief. The problem with stereotypes is that they are often inaccurate and certainly do not apply to all members of the group. Yet, everyone knows their content. Members of the group that is negatively stereotyped feel the pressure, whether or not they endorse the stereotype and whether or not they believe the stereotype applies to them. In chapter 5, we took a long look at research demonstrating the power of stereotype threat—studies that showed the effect of negative stereotypes on minority students' academic performance, female students' mathematics and technology achievements, and White students' accomplishments on athletic tasks.

As Steele (1997) has reminded us, stereotype threat is simply "in the air." It does not originate with any single source—not parents nor teachers nor peers—but rather stems from the general information structures that people have about their social world. Nonetheless, a growing body of research suggests that teachers may hold the key that can activate the antidote to this pernicious problem.

"Wise" Schooling: Providing Feedback to Overcome Threat.   In the movie *Stand and Deliver,* the teacher of a group of Latino students in an inner city high school in Los Angeles, California, challenged his class to take and pass the Advanced Placement exam in calculus. The teacher not only set his expectations very high, but also convinced his students that their mathematical knowledge was expandable beyond what they had allowed themselves to believe. His patient but challenging approach worked. His entire class received AP credit in calculus, an event so unlikely that it prompted the testing agency to question the results. What is most remarkable is that *Stand and Deliver* depicted the true story of teacher Jaime

Escalante (see Mathews, 1988), who refused to allow his Latino students to succumb to the stereotype of inferior scholastic performance. He saw the potential in his students, challenged them to reach it, and convinced them of the truth that their ability would continue to grow as they worked, learned, and persisted.

By "*wise* schooling," Steele specifically refers to education that uses challenge and encouragement to find the essential humanity in people suffering under the threat posed by negative stereotypes. *Challenge* means that teachers establish high standards and expect their students to reach them. *Encouragement* is communicating to students that their intellectual ability is not immutable, but can grow with effort and practice. Jaime Escalante combined these variables and enabled his minority students to become proficient in mathematics. Can we adapt *wise* schooling policies to help women overcome the threat they experience in mathematics, science and technology? Can it help to overcome the digital divide?

Steele (1997) suggests several steps that schools and teachers can use to overcome stereotype threat that we heartily endorse in the context of women and computers. Suggestions include:

• *Stress challenge over remediation.* Girls in computer classes should be given challenging work that shows respect for their abilities and potential. Knowing that girls typically do not perform as well as boys at information technology tasks may prompt teachers to think remedially. Teachers may earnestly think that they should provide easier work so that the girls can "catch up." *Wise* schooling suggests this would be a mistake. People who feel threatened by a negative stereotype need to feel challenged to perform better.

• *Stress the expandability of IT ability.* Girls need to feel that their current performance is not the limit of what they can achieve. Dweck and her colleagues (e.g., Dweck, 1986; Dweck, Chiu, & Hong, 1995) have shown that people differ in their tendency to think that intellectual performance is fixed versus mutable. Situational factors also play a role in this belief. *Wise* education stresses the mutability of intelligence and potential. If women students have spent years in classes feeling anxious about IT and worried about their level of ability, then knowing that their ability can grow with instruction and practice is crucial to overcoming the adverse effects.

• *Value multiple perspectives. Wise* education stresses that there is more than one way to be successful at IT tasks. Recall that in chapter 2, we introduced Turkle and Papert's (1990) observation that females think differently than males about how to approach the challenges in information technology. *Wise* education affirms the diversity of approaches to information technology.

• *Make relevant role models available.* Having women in the roles of computer teacher and computer trouble-shooters offers "existence proofs" to students that negative stereotypes applied to women's capabilities at IT are not insurmountable.

Cohen et al. (1999) adapted two of the most important features of *wise* schooling in a particularly interesting experimental study. Although the content area of their study was not about technology, the research has clear implications for the digital divide. The investigators asked, "How can performance feedback be provided to people suffering from stereotype threat in a way that increases their motivation to do better? How can such feedback strengthen their identification with intellectual domains?" In their study, the stereotyped group was minority students at Stanford University, and the intellectual domain was the students' writing ability.

White and Black students participated in a study in which they were asked to write a letter of recommendation, nominating someone as their favorite teacher, mentor, or coach. They were led to believe that if their essay was sufficiently persuasive, it would be published in a professional journal. A week after writing their nominating essay, they returned to the laboratory and received feedback about their essay. The criticism, presumably written by a White university professor, contained hard-hitting but constructive criticisms ranging from sentence construction to overall impact of the essay. Students were encouraged to revise and resubmit their letters for possible publication.

For some of the students, the criticism was all they received. For other students, the criticism was accompanied by challenge and encouragement—the conditions that comprise the *wise* feedback. The comments made it explicit that if the letter were to be published in the journal, it would have to rise to a higher, more professional standard. It encouraged students by saying, "Remember, I wouldn't go to the trouble of giving you this feedback if I didn't think, based on what I've read in your letter, that you are capable of meeting the higher standard I've mentioned" (Cohen et al., 1999, p. 1306). In a third condition, students were provided with the challenge of the higher standard, asked for a resubmission, but not provided with the encouraging information. Other participants received the criticism without either the challenge or the encouragement. When students were then asked how motivated they were to pursue the writing task for possible publication, White students responded most positively to the challenge; the encouragement about their capabilities was unnecessary. Black students, however, who engage in academic tasks under the pressure of stereotype threat, responded most positively in the *wise* condition. The combination of challenge and encouragement made them more motivated to pursue publishing their article than any other type of feedback.

In the world outside of the laboratory, several universities have implemented novel programs to encourage higher performance by students in traditionally stigmatized groups based on the elements of *wise* schooling. The University of Michigan implemented such a program for minority and non-minority freshmen students. The program emphasizes that it is non-remedial, challenging, and expects high achievement of participants. The program provides enrichment challenges including additional voluntary seminars, extra outside speakers, and discussion groups. Students are encouraged to view their academic potential as expandable. After a semester of participating in the program, minority and White students did very well in their coursework. The effect was most dramatic for minority students, however. Their grades were significantly higher than the grades of minority students who were not in the program, even controlling for previous ability as measured by standardized admissions tests.

There is yet another result from the University of Michigan data that is relevant to the digital divide. In this book, we have seen that even women with excellent GPAs and other indicants of ability to grasp technology still feel anxious and uncomfortable. They underperform at IT tasks and underenroll in IT courses, compared to what one would expect from their level of ability. The same phenomenon typifies the performance of Black students in college (Steele, 1997). Relative to the their high school GPAs and scores on standardized tests, Black students typically attain poorer grades in college courses than do White students with similar high school records and test scores. After participating in the *wise* schooling, the underperformance of Black students at the University of Michigan disappeared (Steele, 1997).

Every teacher in every classroom can apply the *wise* schooling approach. It requires an awareness on the part of teachers and school systems that girls and women are constantly subjected to the pressure of stereotype threat in technology, science, and mathematics. Reducing standards and expectations will not contribute to a solution. Rather, the curriculum must be built upon challenges that raise rather then lower the bar for success, raise expectations for what girls are expected to accomplish, and provide encouragement based on the girls' growing capacity to master technology. This is as true at the kindergarten level as it is at the university. Girls should be expected to work with computers with as much frequency and enthusiasm as boys do, whether it is learning letters from a computer program at age 5 or learning about the growth of dendrites at age 18. Moreover, guidance counselors and administrators need to provide similar wise challenges to girls and women who are choosing their academic courses. Is it all right that high school girls opt out of higher level computer courses (recall Schofield, 1995)? *Wise* schooling says no. The *wise* schooling of the future mandates that girls and women be challenged to improve their computer skills in the most demanding ways provided by the curriculum. With such challenge and encouragement, educators can take major steps to eliminate the gender-based, digital divide.

Teacher Training

We cannot emphasize too strongly the importance of teacher training. School systems spend considerable time and money to provide continuing education and training for teachers. Teacher training in the area of technology is particularly important. Few teachers received substantial education in computers during their own college education and, moreover, the advances in technology are so rapid that training needs to be continual. Every upgrade in computer capability requires training. Every upgrade in the district's operating system requires training. In many school systems, the training in how to use the hardware is available.

However, the digital divide is not a function of the operating system or the size of the computers' RAM. Teachers would welcome and would benefit from school systems providing help and support for overcoming the digital divide. Most teachers are unaware of the problem caused by the selection of software, the structure of the classroom, and the social context of the computing environment. The concepts within the *wise* schooling approach can be taught, but teachers need to be given the opportunity to learn them. We encourage school districts to pay as much attention to the social aspects of computing as they do to the technology hardware. Teacher training is essential to promote awareness of the problem and the tools for overcoming it.

Classroom Structure.   The structure of the classroom, from pre-school to college, is very much determined by the teacher. However, some facets of classroom life affect students' attitudes and behaviors so directly that even the most well-intentioned teacher who monitors his or her own behavior carefully may still structure the classroom in a way that unwittingly contributes to the digital divide.

Attending to the Social Context.   One of the more pervasive antecedents of girls' and women's computer anxiety is the social context in which computing is performed. Throughout this book, we have discussed research showing that girls' IT work and attitudes are markedly affected by the social composition of their learning groups. When girls work in mixed-gender, competitive groups, their computer attitudes become more negative, their anxiety is heightened, and their performance deteriorates.

Research has also shown that, in some circumstances, groups of any kind can be harmful to girls' interest in and ability at computing. Boys often profit from a public social context, but girls do not (Cooper et al., 1990; Robinson-Stavely & Cooper, 1990). This is especially true when the story lines of IT software are oriented toward boys, such as when computer programs use adventure story formats. This research leads us to suggest that classrooms providing private space for individuals to conduct their computing may be beneficial to girls. Allocation of private space can be done in both regular classroom setting or in computer cluster environments. If individualized instruction is attempted, the computing space should be one in which no other students are present. Although it may be expensive to provide private space, it is more costly to the social and economic capital to diminish the computational ability and interest of half of the population.

If the activities and resources make private computing impossible, another possible solution is to use same-sex computer learning groups, in which girls work together on computer problems. Although we hesitate to suggest that computer education necessarily must be segregated by gender, same-sex education is currently a hotly debated issue in education, and in the next chapter we thoroughly examine the pros and cons of separate schooling and/or separate classrooms for girls and boys. To the degree that same-sex learning groups mitigate the anxiety and the competition that arises in mixed-sex groups, we think it is wise to offer girls the opportunity to do their computational learning with children of the same gender.

Fostering Learning by Cooperation: The Jigsaw Classroom.   In addition to private computing and same-sex learning, there is an intriguing alternative approach that, used in conjunction with the suggestions on social context, may be able to reduce anxiety and overcome some of the other adverse consequences of public, mixed-gender contexts: Make both sexes integral to solving a problem through interdependent computer tasks. This approach holds promise as a way to both mitigate computer anxiety and lead girls and young women to feel a sense of identification with and ownership of technology. Mixed-sex groups in computer contexts present three major problems, all of which are related to boys' greater experience with computers: computer anxiety, gender-based exclusion, and too much helping. If classes are planned to circumvent these problems, then boys and girls may be able to work together in a way that will benefit both sexes.

Studies of cooperative learning techniques show that cooperative strategies can be effective not only in facilitating learning, but also in increasing feelings of inclusion and cooperation among diverse groups of students (Johnson, Maruyama, Johnson, Nelson, & Skon, 1981; Johnson & Johnson, 1989; U.S. Department of Education, 1992). More than 60 studies, many conducted by research centers sponsored by the federal government or by local school districts, show that when teachers structure their classroom assignments such that all students are integral to solving common problems (interdependent goals) and each student has individual accountability, students' achievement goes up. Since they focus students on teamwork and cooperation, rather than competition, cooperative learning environments also provide a more comfortable working environment, one that will likely reduce computer anxiety.

A widely used cooperative strategy that is particularly useful in the context of teaching technology is the Jigsaw Classroom. Designed by Elliot Aronson and his graduate students at the University of Texas (E. Aronson et al., 1978), Jigsaw classes are constructed so that the individual students must rely on each other when completing classroom assignments. In contrast to the more traditional competitive learning environments, the interdependent focus of the Jigsaw strategy ensures that all students in a classroom participate equally in learning as they work together as a cooperative group to complete classroom assignments.

In Jigsaw classrooms, students are assigned to small groups of about four members, and each group should be mixed with regard to race, gender and ability. Each group of students is then given an assignment that has been divided into four unique and non-overlapping parts. Individual group members take one of the parts as their personal assignment. This way, each student is responsible for one piece of his or her group's assignment, and each piece has equal importance in the completion of the group assignment. Once students are assigned their individual parts, they become their group's "expert" on that topic, and are allowed to consult with other "experts" who have been assigned the same piece in the other groups. For instance, if the group project was to design a web page, one student may be in charge of figuring out how to import photographs to the page, another may be in charge of writing the text of the page, another may be in charge of learning to insert a button to collect data from web visitors, and another may be assigned the task of learning how to change the font and style of the page.

After students have completed their portion of the assignment, they return to their original group to present their work. At that time, the members within each group must work together to integrate each member's individual piece into the final group assignment. To return to our web page design scenario, once the students convene as a group, they must assemble the different pieces they have learned into a larger whole, the page itself. Because each individual group member is the only one in the group who has knowledge about his or her individual piece, he or she must teach it to the other group members. The interdependence among students fosters collaboration rather than competition among the group members. It is in each group's best interest if all of its members succeed. Excluding members is not beneficial because each group member suffers if one of their peers does not do well on his or her part.

An important aspect of Jigsaw learning is that students are tested on all of the aspects of the topic area. For this reason, they must rely on the other members of their group when completing the assignment or learning the material. Grading may be done on the group level, as in a group project grade, or the individual level, as in an individual quiz, but students must learn the information for each piece of the project.

Overall, tests of the Jigsaw method and other cooperative learning techniques have shown positive results (Aronson, 1992). Jigsaw methods promote discussion among the group members and foster participation and contribution from all students. After working in interdependent groups, students report greater liking for school and also report higher levels of self-esteem. Students also report better relationships with their peers, shown by increased liking for their classmates. Importantly, the increased liking among classmates appears to reduce intergroup conflict, as students' increased liking spans gender and racial boundaries. Also, the increased feelings of acceptance and inclusion in Jigsaw classes leads previously poorly performing students to show more improvement than they do in more traditional classes.

We believe that girls and young women may receive similar benefits if Jigsaw methods are used in computer classes. If girls and young women feel included in computer learning rather than left with the feeling that the course is really not for people like them, they will be more likely to identify with the topic, enjoy the course more and show superior performance.

One reason why Jigsaw learning may work especially well with computer lessons is the widely varying skills students bring to computer classrooms. Some students may enter the classroom more familiar with programming tasks than others. Instead of being bored while waiting for the other students to catch up, Jigsaw classes provide a structure in which advanced students can essentially become "teachers" and help their peers with less sophisticated skills. As girls and boys learn from each other in their expert groups, they can utilize the knowledge of their fellow students as a resource for more basic questions. The classroom teacher is then freed to spend time answering more sophisticated questions, and to monitor the group learning situation to make sure that no student is having difficulty completing the basics of his or her assignment. The fact that each student is ultimately responsible for relaying her or his knowledge back to their group, ensures that each student learn the material well enough to "teach" it to their peers.

Cooperative learning techniques such as the Jigsaw method may also go a long way toward alleviating computer anxiety. Because the students have their expert groups to consult with and fall back on, cooperative learning may help dispel the anxiety that often accompanies computer use. Instead of being forced to compete for the attention of a busy teacher or to compete with other students to see who can finish the fastest, students are encouraged to use their fellow students as a resource, thus potentially alleviating their arousal and anxiety.

Overall, the research strongly suggests that the Jigsaw method and other cooperative learning techniques do admirably well in increasing student performance and providing a comfortable classroom environment. We think that such learning strategies will be productive in helping young women identify with computers and overcome the anxiety that some feel when performing computer tasks.

We believe that adoption of the suggestions outlined in this chapter can go a long way toward increasing girls' and young women's identification with computers and making them feel more comfortable when using IT. Parents and teachers alike must be vigilant in assessing the way that their interactions may affect girls' and young women's attitudes toward computers. Challenging girls to develop positive expectations for themselves at crucial ages, providing them with the opportunities for learning about computers in environments that lessen anxiety, and paying attention to the factors that lead to disidentification will be crucial factors in giving girls a vision of how IT may benefit them in the future.

7

Solutions: Single-Sex Schools and Classrooms?

Of all the solutions proposed to remedy the gender gap in science and technology, none has generated more controversy than the fierce and often emotional debate over single-sex education. And all signs suggest that the controversy will continue to rage on in the months and years to come. The U.S. Department of Education recently announced a plan to amend the Title IX section of the Education Amendment of 1972. Title IX is the section that prohibits federally funded programs from excluding students because of their gender. It ensures, for instance, that girls and boys in public schools have equal access to athletic programs. And to this point, most have viewed it as prohibiting federally funded single-sex schools. The new changes, supported by Senators Hillary Rodham Clinton, Kay Bailey Hutchison, and other key female and male politicians, center around single-sex education. In its own words, the purpose of the amendment is "... to provide more flexibility for educators to establish single-sex classes and schools at the elementary and secondary levels."

In the past several decades in the United States, experimentation with single-sex education has been largely confined to private school environments. Of the 89,508 operating public elementary and secondary schools in the country, only 11 are currently single sex. Some attribute public schools' reluctance to experiment with single-sex education to administrators' fear of sex discrimination lawsuits based on Title IX. The new amendment will likely open the floodgates and ensure that single-sex options are more widely available in public school settings. In fact, the new amendment, if passed, may dramatically change the structure of public school classrooms as we know them.

Is single-sex schooling really the solution to remedying the science and technology gender gap? Some parents seem to think so. A glance at the statistics surrounding single-sex schools at the elementary and secondary levels indicates a renewed interest in single-sex education. Applications to single-sex schools increased 40% from the period 1991 to 2000 (National Coalition of Girls' Schools, Fall Data Survey, 2000), and 31 new single-sex schools opened in the country between 1997 and 2002. At the same time that many have showed a renewed interest in single-sex education, a number of organizations, among them the American Association of University Women (AAUW), have spoken out in favor of co-education (AAUW, 1998b). The popular media has been following the debate by reporting on case studies, research, and the philosophical positions held by notable public figures as well as parents and teachers directly involved in the schools. The reports reflect the wide range of opinions that exists both in the academic community and in the public sphere.

Many reports espouse what appear to be remarkable benefits of single-sex schooling. Consider the Young Women's Leadership School of East Harlem, for instance. The Young Women's Leadership School is a public all-girls secondary school located in East Harlem, New York (Haberman, 2001). The experimental school was created in 1996; although it is public, it was helped along by a large financial contribution from philanthropist Ann Tisch. The Young Women's Leadership School is the first single-sex *public* school to operate in New York since the 1970s, and its purpose is to provide young women from Harlem a chance to focus on their studies without the distraction of boys. So far, the school has been a great success. Most students at the Young Women's Leadership School are from demographic groups that usually underperform academically. For instance, the large majority of students come from economically disadvantaged backgrounds; almost 75% of the class of 2001 came from families classified as below the poverty line. The school also reflects Harlem's racial composition—over 95% of the students are Black or Latina.

Students at this school have beaten the socio-structural odds. Students at the Young Women's Leadership School dramatically outperform their peers at co-educational public schools. Last year, 100% of the students at the Young Women's Leadership School passed the English part of the New York Regents exam, in comparison to only 42% of New York City students overall. All but one of the young women in the class of 2001 was accepted to a 4-year college, even though a full 90% were the first member of their family to attend college. There is no question that the experience was a dramatic success for the students. Still, some have questioned whether the single-sex environment is responsible for the students' academic success or instead, whether the academic performance differences are attributable to the financial support, good teachers, and small classes provided by the school.

Other highly publicized experiments in single-sex education also appear successful, at least anecdotally. The Seattle Girls' School (SGS), an all-girls middle school focused on math and science education, is another school that has received recent media attention (Cleary, 2002). The Seattle Girls School (SGS) is an example of single-sex experimentation in the private sphere. Started in 2001 with a $500,000 seed grant from the Bill and Melinda Gates Foundation, the school's mission is to encourage young women to participate in the sciences. Teachers, parents, and students affiliated with the school report that the all-girls environment allows young women to focus on academics without the distraction of boys. They feel that the all-girls environment empowers young women to pursue and succeed at careers in traditionally male-dominated fields such as mathematics and science.

And the list goes on. The students at Western High, an all-girls public school in Baltimore, like students at the Young Women's Leadership School, come from economically and racially diverse backgrounds; more than one third met the school district's qualifications for subsidized lunches. Regardless, the young women at this school consistently outperform other students in their school district on a battery of important academic outcome variables. In 2001, their average SAT scores were more than 100 points higher than the district-wide average. Western High students also took more Advanced Placement examinations than did students at any of the other schools in their district, and over 90% of the class of 2001 attended college directly after high school graduation.

Young men can also derive benefits from single-sex environments. Although a lawsuit prevented it from continuing on as a single-sex school in the mid-1990s, the Malcolm X Academy, an all-boys school in Detroit for young Black American men, seemed to be very successful in improving the outcomes of this disadvantaged group. Seventh graders at Malcolm X Academy had the highest mathematics scores of 77 Detroit schools, and the second highest scores of Michigan's 780 schools.

Despite these highly publicized positive outcomes, not everyone agrees that single-sex schools are the best option for students. Perhaps the most vivid evidence of controversy occurred soon after the Young Women's Leadership School of East Harlem opened its doors to their first class of young women. Almost immediately, both the New York chapter of the American Civil Liberties Union (ACLU) and the National Organization of Women (NOW) filed lawsuits against the school, arguing that it should be closed immediately because it violated the "equal access" clause of Title IX. Although to date the Young Women's Leadership School is still open, similar lawsuits forced the Malcolm X Academy to go co-educational. Are the positions of NOW and ACLU the bastions of civil rights and equal opportunity, or are they striking a blow against the most radical and effective attempts to break down the racial and gender barriers? Apart from the prescriptions and proscriptions of Title IX and other Constitutional issues, we need to address the question of what is gained and what is lost from an educational perspective if children are taught in single-sex environments.

Some believe that single-sex education may be used as a "band aid" approach to remedy problems in our education system that should demand longer term solutions—problems such as securing better training for teachers in all school districts, instituting smaller class sizes, spending money on better facilities, and working to improve student discipline. Co-education advocates note that many of the successful single-sex programs differ from the standard schools not only in their sex composition, but also in their smaller teacher–student ratios overall, smaller classes, and superior facilities. They attribute the incredible success of students to these structural factors rather than gender separation per se. Others decry the fact that single-sex schools encourage segregation. They wonder why educators in the first decade of the 21st century would start revisiting the idea of sex segregation 30 years after Equal Rights Amendment supporters struggled to make all public school facilities equally accessible to both boys and girls.

Others believe that co-educational settings may help young men and women prepare for the future by providing important social benefits. That is, students in co-educational elementary and secondary schools may become better prepared for a mixed-sex professional and family life. This position was elaborated in an *Atlantic Monthly* article questioning the benefits of single-sex schooling (Kaminer, 1998). The author, herself a graduate of an all-women's college, questioned whether single-sex schools did not hurt women's social and personal development in the long run. Still others argue that rather than dispelling gender stereotypes, single-sex schools may end up encouraging them.

In this chapter, we analyze the benefits and drawbacks of single-sex education as a solution to the gender equity problem in science and technology. Single-sex education is both an extremely important issue and a very complicated one. It is also a timely issue. With the revisions to Title IX, federal, state, and local governments will soon face important decisions about how to structure not only classes, but also schools themselves. As parents and educators, we must be cognizant of the issues so that we can make the best decisions for the students of today and tomorrow. Our intention is not to solve this important question in this chapter, but rather to inform the debate. There are important lessons to be learned from the research and from the ideas that are currently being debated. We know that a greater understanding and knowledge of the issues can give us insight into how to provide young women with more opportunities to learn about and benefit from computers, technology, and science.

THE SINGLE-SEX/CO-EDUCATION DEBATE

Educators, scholars, parents, and students argue for the co-educational status quo for any of a number of philosophical and political reasons. Some co-education advocates question whether single-sex education benefits students academically at all. Rather, they think that the studies showing superior education benefits for single-sex schools and class-rooms are flawed in important ways. Others acknowledge that there may be some educational benefits, but think that they are outweighed by the social drawbacks of single-sex settings. Still other co-education propo-nents advocate the status quo for philosophical reasons. They argue that sex-segregated schooling is regressive. Important gains have been made in the past 40 years in gender equality in education. For instance, the last strongholds of sex segregation, like the Virginia Military Institute, have been eradicated. In their opinion, the drawbacks of sex segregation, like racial segregation, outweigh the potential educational benefits that may be realized in single-sex settings. A deeper analysis of the positions both in favor and against single-sex schooling shows some important facts, and we discuss the two positions in more detail in the next section.

Why Might Single-Sex Schools Be Superior?

Proponents of single-sex schools argue that putting boys and girls together in the classroom is detrimental for students, and particularly detrimental for girls. One reason for this claim is based on the *activation of stereotypes* when gender is a focal issue. Having boys and girls together in the same school keeps the cognitive representation of gender in the forefront. In a co-educational environment, boys' facility and experience with technol-ogy and their skill at math and science encourages positive attitudes and higher performance. For girls, co-education in technology, math, and sci-ence brings anxiety, negative attitudes, and inhibited performance. Acti-vating the gender concept makes it more probable that teachers will inadvertently select male-oriented software and examples for their com-puter classrooms. Moreover, highlighting gender will allow that "threat in the air" to place its heavy burden on the girls in the school, whether they believe the social stereotype or not.

The increased spotlight on gender may also draw attention to sex roles and sex stereotypes. This may encourage both females and males to pur-sue more sex-stereotyped courses of study, either because they think of themselves in more gendered terms, or in order to fit in with their peers. If females and males choose areas of study based on gender stereotyped roles, this will contribute to the gender disparities seen in the higher education and employment sector (Carpenter & Hayden, 1987).

Social Concerns. A second class of reasons that supports single-sex education stems from the social concerns of both boys and girls. Proponents point out that students have only limited time and attention that they can allocate to either academic or social concerns. Co-educational settings presumably shift students' attention away from the academic sphere to the social sphere. Boys and girls, particularly in the middle and high school years, may be distracted from their studies by concerns about their popularity, appearance, and relationships. Co-education has to fight through the social relationships to convince students to focus on their education rather than each other. Proponents of this argument conclude that single-sex education will be equally beneficial for boys and for girls, relative to the typical co-educational alternative.

Teacher Attention. Other arguments favoring single-sex education draw directly from classroom observation research. As we noted in the previous chapter, boys in mixed-sex classrooms receive more classroom resources than girls (AAUW, 1998a; Burger & Sandy, 1998; Sadker & Sadker, 1994). Without being aware of it, teachers give boys more attention and more constructive encouragement than they give girls in the same classrooms. As a result, girls learn less course material and feel less confident about their academic performance than boys. Advocates of single-sex education claim that separating the sexes will minimize these factors. If so, single-sex settings at crucial times in students' academic self-concept development may help to remedy the current gender inequalities in science and computer attitudes and achievement.

Student Interaction Patterns. Interaction patterns of the students themselves may also create an uneven playing field for girls. Although males and females appear to have similar personality types, sex differences nonetheless arise when children interact in mixed-sex contexts (Maccoby, 1990). And these sex differences appear to benefit boys. Jacklin and Maccoby (1978), for instance, had girls interact with other students in pairs. The girls were paired either with a boy or with another girl. The researchers then timed how long each child sat back and looked on as their partner played with the toys. When the girls were paired with other girls, they rarely sat by and watched as the other played. Thus, the researchers concluded that girls are not less assertive or inactive by nature. However, girls in mixed-sex pairs tended to defer to their male partners. These girls spent a significant amount of time sitting by and watching as their male partners took over control of the toys.

Other studies have corroborated the findings that when boys and girls interact in mixed-sex settings, boys tend to dominate the available resources. Powlishta (1987, cited in Maccoby, 1990), for instance, studied what happened when mixed-sex pairs were left alone in a playroom with an attractive toy. When the pairs were left unsupervised, boys ended up spending more time with the toy than the girls. Gender differences in interaction styles may be the reason why boys tend to take over resources in mixed-sex settings. Girls interacting in cooperative activities tend to use polite suggestions to get their opinions and desires across (Maccoby, 1990). In contrast, boys of the same age tend to use direct commands to achieve their goals. Research shows that boys begin to ignore or discount girls' polite suggestions around the time that the children are about to enter school (Maccoby, 1990; Serbin, Sprafkin, Elman, & Doyle, 1982).

The developmental psychologist Eleanor Maccoby (1990) concludes that many of the gender differences in interaction styles have their roots in the rules and norms that develop in children's playgroups when they are very young. Children spend much of their time in sex-segregated playgroups, and the playgroups for each gender develop different norms for interactions. Boys in same-sex groups tend to use direct speaking styles, tend to interrupt each other more in conversation, and more often refuse to obey each others' orders than girls in same-sex groups. In contrast, interactions within all-girl groups tend to be focused more on relationships. Girls tend to be more polite in their interactions with each other, they tend to wait patiently for other group members to finish speaking before interrupting, and they tend to suggest rather than command (Maccoby, 1990). Some researchers have referred to the different norms that arise in different sex playgroups as distinct "cultures" (Maccoby, 1990).

Boys and girls grow accustomed to their typical playgroup interaction styles. But the styles females have learned may put them at a disadvantage when members of the two "cultures" meet and engage in mixed-sex interaction. For this reason, girls interacting in mixed-sex settings may end up contributing less to group discussions in school. In mixed gender computer and mathematics classes, and girls and young women do not participate as actively as their male peers. To the degree that "hands on" learning leads to more positive computer attitudes and performance, girls in mixed-sex settings will be disadvantaged. In light of the research on teacher attention and students' interaction patterns, some proponents of single-sex schools argue that although co-education looks like "equal access" on the outside, the classroom dynamics it engenders makes it not equal in reality. They believe that girls will benefit from, and become empowered in, environments where they are not competing with boys for classroom resources.

Role Models. Another argument in favor of single-sex schooling is that they tend to provide more same-sex role models in instructional roles in math, science, and computer classes than do mixed-sex environments (Miller-Bernal, 1993). Note that it is not necessary for the teachers in same-sex schools to be of the same gender as their pupils. Nonetheless, same-sex schools tend to have a higher proportion of instructors of the relevant gender. Some have argued that male teachers may be more likely than female ones to make stereotypic inferences about female students, and thus may end up dissuading female students either consciously or unconsciously from pursuing study in traditionally male-dominated topics. Female teachers in topics such as math, science, and computers may also help to break down the sex-stereotypes that surround these topics of study. Research suggests that female role models have positive effects on female employees (Geis, Boston, & Hoffman, 1985), and some have argued that female teachers in areas like math, science, and computers will lead to similar positive outcomes.

It thus seems that there are five major reasons that girls, in particular, may benefit from single-sex schools:

1. Single-sex schools allow students to focus more exclusively on academics because they provide fewer social distractions.
2. Single-sex schools may lessen students' adoption of sex-stereotyped preferences.
3. Single-sex schools may alleviate problems of sex-skewed classroom resource allocation.
4. Single-sex schools may allow students to participate more equally at crucial points in their academic self-concept development.
5. Single-sex schools tend to provide more same-sex role models, which may help to break down sex stereotypes and alleviate problems of tokenism.

Co-education Proponents

On the other side of the fierce controversy are proponents of the co-education status quo. These educators and researchers argue that co-educational settings are superior to single-sex ones for a number of reasons, including:

1. Mixed-sex schools more accurately reflect the reality of the social world. Thus, they do the best job of preparing students for the fu-

ture where they will inevitably face a mixed-sex workplace, family life, and social life.

2. Rather than dispelling gender stereotypes, sex segregation in schools may actually inadvertently reinforce them by drawing students' and teachers' attention to the idea that there are gender differences in interests and learning styles.

3. Segregating students by sex may put young women in victim roles. Perhaps students will infer that girls have their own class or school because they have inferior academic skills and ability.

RESEARCH ON SINGLE-SEX SCHOOLS
VERSUS MIXED-SEX SCHOOLS

Throughout this volume, we have relied heavily on empirical research to raise questions and suggest answers. In this section, we examine studies that have compared students attending single-sex versus co-educational schools on a number of important academic outcome variables. We will see whether type of school appears to influence students' attitudes toward math, science, and technology, their academic confidence in these areas, the degree to which they endorse gender stereotypes, and their academic performance. We will also look at whether type of school impacts students' plans for the future, such as their anticipated career choices.

The research comparing girls' and boys' outcomes as a function of school type is extensive, and the findings are not always completely consistent across studies. One reason for the inconsistencies is, in many cases, the single-sex schools studied differ from the co-educational control schools in important ways beyond the single-sex/co-educational variable of interest. For example, most single-sex schools in the United States are private, and vary in their selectivity in accepting applicants. In order to test whether the sex composition of the school is responsible for any differences in student performance, confidence, or future professional choices, researchers must find co-educational control schools that are equally selective, and are also similar on other important variables such as family income, race, and so on. In addition to these methodological difficulties, there may be important demographic differences in the type of parents that send their children to single-sex versus mixed-sex schools. These sorts of pre-existing demographic differences can influence students' confidence, achievement, and plans for the future in systematic ways. Most of the studies we review here pay as careful attention as possible to these issues and attempt to control for extraneous factors like pre-existing demographic differences between students in single-sex and co-educational schools in their analyses. However, the control procedures are not always perfect, which sometimes leave results open to interpretation. Despite the important methodological issues that arise when comparing self-selected groups, we believe that the research is informative and important and, when examined critically and taken as a whole, we think it can give us clues about how to increase young women's opportunities in science and technology.

Much of the research on single-sex schools was designed to analyze students' performance and attitudes about math and science. Although technology brings with it additional dimensions that are troubling to females, such as the sex-stereotyping of the IT software, most of the data about attitudes and performance in the male-stereotyped domains of math and science apply equally well to computer attitudes, confidence, and performance (Clarke & Chambers, 1989; Collis, 1987).

Attitudes, Academic Self-Esteem, Academic Confidence

Do young women who attend single-sex schools feel more positively toward math, science, and technology than young women attending co-educational schools? Some reports suggest that single-sex environments do provide academic advantages to girls beyond those provided by co-educational environments (see Mael, 1998 for a review of the research). If single-sex schools lead young women to form more positive attitudes toward computers, math, and science and lead them to express increased confidence in their abilities in those traditionally sex-typed fields, this might be a first step in encouraging them to study these topics at the collegiate or graduate level.

Some studies show that young women attending all-girls secondary schools hold more positive attitudes toward traditionally male-dominated topics of study than young women of the same age attending co-educational schools. Gwizdala and Steinback (1990), for example, surveyed 722 young women attending either a single-sex or a co-educational college preparatory school. Their study showed that students at the all-girls school held more positive attitudes toward mathematics in general and more positive attitudes toward their own ability in mathematics than students attending the co-educational comparison school. The all-girls school students also reported more comfort when asking questions in their math classes than co-educational school students. When asked how they would feel about learning in a mixed-sex setting, the young women at the all-girls school reported that they thought their performance would suffer in co-educational classes.

Other studies also show that young women attending all-girls schools have more positive attitudes toward math and the physical sciences than girls at co-educational schools. In fact, research looking at both boys' and girls' attitudes as a function of type of school shows an interesting pattern.

Co-educational settings seem to lead students to hold attitudes that are in line with the gender stereotypes of the area of study. Young men in co-educational schools hold more positive attitudes toward, and feel more confident in, their abilities in traditionally male-dominated fields like math and physical science. In contrast, young women in co-educational settings tend to report more positive attitudes and confidence in traditionally female sex-typed areas like English and biology. There is some indication that single-sex settings minimize the effects of these gender stereotypes. Young women in single-sex schools are more positive toward and more confident in traditionally male sex-typed areas of study compared to their female peers at co-educational schools. In contrast, young men are less favorable toward and confident in traditionally male sex-typed areas of study than are their male peers in co-educational schools.

Lawrie and Brown (1992) surveyed 284 British students aged 14–15 in order to assess how school type impacted their attitudes toward mathematics. Their study showed that single-sex environments were beneficial to girls, but that mixed-sex environments were slightly more beneficial to boys. Girls attending the all-girls school reported enjoying math significantly more than a control group of girls attending a co-educational school. Girls in the single-sex environment also reported that they found math less difficult than girls in co-educational schools, although this difference did not reach statistical significance. The pattern for boys was somewhat different. Type of school did not impact boys' reported enjoyment of math. However, boys attending the all-boys school reported more difficulty with math than did boys attending the mixed school. The pattern of attitude scores indicates that girls' outcomes improve when boys are not in the school, but that boys may actually benefit from having girls in the school. One possibility is that boys receive advantages from being labeled a "male" in mixed-sex environments. Since the stereotypes benefit boys in math, they might think of themselves as having more ability when their sex is made salient by the presence of girls in the classroom. Boys in all-boys schools, however, receive no benefits from the positive male stereotypes because they apply to all the students in the school.

Lawrie and Brown also looked at whether school type was correlated with students' intentions to pursue study of various academic topics in the future. To test this, they asked students to indicate in which subjects they would take A-level examinations (competitive exams) if they remained in school for the following year (see Fig. 7.1). Results showed a similar pattern to the attitude items described already. Girls attending the all-girls schools were more than twice as likely to predict taking A-levels in math (14.7%) than were girls in the mixed school (6.7%). Girls in the mixed school, on the other hand, were more likely to express interest in taking English A-levels (26%) than were girls in the single-sex school (16.3%). Re-

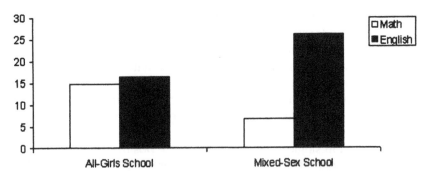

FIG. 7.1. Percentage of girls choosing to take examinations in math and English depending on type of school attended (adapted from Lawrie & Brown, 1992).

sults from the boys were the opposite. Boys at the all-boys schools indicated less interest in the physics A-levels (9%) than did boys attending the co-educational school (23%), but were more interested in the languages A-levels (17%), a traditionally female sex-typed area of study, than their same-sex counterparts attending mixed schools (6%).

Thus, the Lawrie and Brown (1992) study suggests that the gender composition of the school interacts with sex-typed areas of study. Boys and girls in mixed-sex settings tend to like topics that are sex typed for their gender. In contrast, single-sex settings appear to provide some respite from rigid gender stereotyping. Girls tend to like math and physical science more, and boys tend to like traditional female topics more, under single-sex conditions.

Harvey and Stables (1986) focused on the benefits of same-sex schooling for the physical sciences. They surveyed 2,300 students at single- and mixed-sex schools in southwest England about their attitudes toward various scientific disciplines. The pattern of results for science attitudes paralleled those found by Lawrie and Brown (1992) for math attitudes. Girls at all-girls schools were more positive toward science in general, and physics and chemistry in particular, than girls attending mixed-sex schools. Results for attitudes toward biology, a traditionally female discipline, showed an advantage in favor of mixed-sex settings. Although boys' attitudes toward science in general or chemistry in particular did not differ by type of school, their attitudes toward physics paralleled those found by Lawrie and Brown (1992). Boys attending mixed-sex schools had more positive attitudes toward physics than boys in all boys' schools. In contrast, single-sex settings lessened the stereotyped behavior. Boys attending all-boys schools had more positive attitudes toward the traditionally female discipline of biology than did boys in mixed-sex schools.

Other studies also offer support for the notion that young women attending all-girls schools have more positive attitudes toward math and science than same-sex peers attending co-educational schools. Colley et al. (1994) asked students to indicate preferences for areas of study. Results from students in the 11–12 age group showed that girls attending single-sex schools showed stronger preferences for math and science than same-aged peers attending co-educational schools. Boys attending single-sex schools showed stronger preferences for music and art than boys attending co-educational schools.

Another important outcome variable measured in the research is academic self-esteem or academic self-confidence. Research shows that young women's choices about future coursework choices and career choices are influenced by their confidence. Therefore, it is important to know whether type of school influences academic self-esteem and self-confidence. Cairns (1990) suggested that young women attending single-sex schools may be more academically self-confident than those attending mixed-sex schools. He surveyed middle school students attending academically focused single-sex and mixed-sex schools in Ireland. Results from his study showed that young women attending the single-sex schools had higher levels of academic self-esteem and stronger internal loci of control than a group of same-aged peers who attended co-educational schools, even when the two groups were equated on their socioeconomic backgrounds.

Girls' *overall* sense of self-esteem at all-girls schools is roughly similar to girls' overall sense of self-esteem in co-educational environments (Brutsaert & Bracke, 1994). Considering Cairns' finding with middle school girls, the most likely conclusion is that girls at all-girls and co-educational schools achieve their self-worth through different avenues. Consistent with this notion, Granleese and Joseph (1993) found that girls at mixed-sex schools achieved their sense of self-worth primarily from their physical appearance, whereas the sense of self-worth of girls at single-sex schools appeared to be driven by their own behavioral conduct.

Single-Sex Schools and Computers

Jones and Clarke (1995) asked young women enrolled in single-sex and co-educational schools in Victoria, Australia, about their attitudes toward computers. They predicted that girls in all-girls schools would have more positive attitudes about computers than their counterparts who had learned about computers in mixed-sex schools. Results from their study strongly supported their prediction: Students in all-girls settings had both more positive affect toward computers and more positive thoughts about computers than girls attending mixed schools.

Jones and Clarke (1995) explored *why* girls in the all-girls schools had more positive attitudes toward computers by looking more closely at their survey data. One possibility that would be consistent with some of the other observations that we reported earlier is that girls at single-sex schools had more access to computers than girls in mixed-sex schools. At least in the Victoria sample, that turned out *not* to be the case. Girls at both types of schools reported approximately the same level of access to, and equal amounts of time on, computers. The intriguing finding in Jones and Clarke's data was that girls in the all girls' schools reported having *more varied experiences* with computers and reported learning about computers from more sources than their counterparts at mixed-sex schools. Their analyses showed that students' diversity of computer experience, rather than their overall computing time, was the best predictor of positive computer attitudes.

From their data and their observations, Jones and Clarke speculated that girls may have more varied experiences with information technology because of the phenomenon that fosters boys' greater access to teacher time. As we noted earlier, in mixed-sex classrooms, boys dominate the teachers' time and teachers are more attentive to boys' questions and comments. Jones and Clarke reasoned that this dynamic might lead girls in co-educational classes to spend more time working quietly on tasks with which they are already familiar rather than venturing out to learn new programs and applications. Consequently, girls in mixed-sex settings may spend a lot of time at the computer, but not receive much diverse experience. Perhaps girls in single-sex settings, on the other hand, feel freer to explore novel programs and applications and thus end up with more varied experiences. Although this is conjecture at this point, it does explain the pattern of results obtained by Jones and Clarke (1995) with an explanation supported by previous research.

Overall, research suggests that same-sex schooling offers benefits for girls and young women in terms of their attitudes toward traditionally male-oriented subjects like technology, science, and math. There is less agreement about the effect of same-sex schools on the academic accomplishments of boys and girls. Our next section explores this crucial question.

Academic Performance: Research Supporting the Benefits of Same-Sex Education

In this section, we examine whether permitting Jared and Martha to attend boy-only and girl-only schools will benefit either of their academic achievements. Young and Fraser's (1990) analysis of 3,638 ninth-grade students in Australia showed that young women attending single-sex schools performed better academically than their female counterparts who were attending co-educational schools. These performance differences held even when the students at the two types of schools were matched for their socioeconomic background (see also Riordan, 1990). Other research has also shown evidence that single-sex schools may provide potential academic performance benefits. Lee and Lockheed (1990), for instance, showed in a sample of more than 1,000 students that young women attending single-sex schools demonstrated superior mathematics achievement and viewed mathematics less gender stereotypically than their female counterparts who attended co-educational schools. The benefits of all-girls schooling remained even after the researchers controlled for student background characteristics and school characteristics. In contrast, boys in co-educational schools outperformed boys in single-sex settings.

In another study on type of school and achievement, Carpenter and Hayden (1987) surveyed students in single-sex and mixed-sex public schools in Victoria, Australia. Results showed that girls attending public all-girls schools achieved more academically and were more likely to take a science course in their final year of high school than were girls attending co-educational public institutions..

Results from studies looking at single-sex colleges have also shown academic advantages. Smith (1990), for instance, found that women attending single-sex colleges graduated at a higher rate than those attending co-educational institutions even after controlling for factors such as high school GPA, parents' education and income, SAT scores, and ethnic background.

Academic Performance: The Nonsignificant Findings

As is clear from the preceding review, there have been several studies documenting academic performance benefits of single-sex education for young women in attitudes, and achievements in subjects that have been traditionally male dominated such as the physical sciences, mathematics, and computer science. However, as we noted at the beginning of the chapter, the results looking at the relationship between school type and academic performance are not completely consistent in the literature. Several studies showed no differences in attitudes or academic performance as a function of type of school attended. Signorella, Frieze, and Hershey (1996), for instance, showed that the degree to which young women subscribed to gender stereotypes did not differ as a function of whether they attended a single-sex or mixed-sex school. Similarly, Marsh (1989) reported no significant differences in performance variables between students attending single-sex versus co-educational schools. Another recent study, conducted by LePore and Warren (1997), using data from the National Educational Longitudinal Study of 1988, failed to find differences in academic performance or in overall self-esteem between young women who attended single-sex or co-educational Catholic schools. Their study also showed that the academic performance and self-esteem of young men did not differ as a function of type of school. Carpenter and Hayden's (1987) previously reported finding of an advantage for same-sex education in Australian public schools was not replicated in a companion study of Australian same-sex vs. co-educational *private* schools.

We should not be dismayed by some studies finding differences as a function of type of school and other studies showing no differences. One important reason for conflicting results has to do with the methodological shortcomings that are in intrinsic to studying groups that are not randomly assigned to conditions (Marsh, 1991). As we pointed out earlier in this chapter, the students who attend single-sex schools may be different, or their parents may be different, in important ways relative to students who attend mixed-sex schools. Other reasons for the inconsistent findings are that single-sex and mixed-sex schools are considerably variable in and of themselves. Some schools are more academically rigorous and focused than others. Some are private and some are public; some are religious and some are secular. It is thus difficult to find perfect control groups against which to measure the attitudinal and performance variables. Nonetheless, we hope the differences in previous studies will inspire more ingenious research methodologies that can overcome these intrinsic design difficulties.

GENDER-STEREOTYPED CONCEPTIONS OF MATHEMATICS AND SCIENCE

Another way that single-sex schools could be beneficial to their students is through decreasing their gender stereotypes about the appropriateness of males and females participating in traditionally sex-typed areas of study and fields of interest. If young women have fewer gender stereotypic conceptions of the types of people who study math, science, and technology, they may personally feel that they have more choice in pursuing courses in those areas. Researchers have noted that one way single-sex schools break up gender stereotypes is through the gender of the faculty member teaching computer, math, and science-related courses. For instance, all-girls schools tend to have more women faculty that can serve as role models and examples for young women wishing to pursue computers, math, and science in college or as a career.

Although there is no work to date on type of school and its effect on gender stereotyping of computer use or computer science, some studies suggest that students attending single-sex schools hold fewer gender stereotypic conceptions of math and science study than their same-aged counterparts attending co-educational schools. Stables (1990), for instance, showed that students in co-educational schools had more sex-stereotypic perceptions of attitudes regarding courses of study than comparable students attending single-sex schools. Lee and Lockheed (1990) found that girls attending single-sex schools viewed mathematics less gender stereotypically than their counterparts who attended co-educational schools.

Some work even indicates that students attending single-sex schools may even end up with less sex-stereotypic conceptions of men's and women's places in society. Lee and Marks (1990), for instance, conducted a 6-year longitudinal study with a sample of 1,533 college students who had either attended Catholic single-sex high schools or Catholic co-educational high schools. They were particularly interested in investigating the long-term effects of attending one type of school over the other, so they surveyed the students 4 years after high school as they were graduating from college. Results indicated that young women who had attended single-sex schools showed evidence of less stereotypic attitudes about females in the workplace than those who had attended co-educational schools (see also Lee & Bryk, 1986).

The lessened stereotypic attitudes about women in the workplace that were held by young women who had attended all-girls high schools is an important finding. Perhaps single-sex settings, or factors present in single-sex settings, help to foster less gender-stereotypic conceptions of men and women. Perhaps attending a school where male–female interactions were not as salient may benefit women by letting them arrive at their own conceptions of females' abilities and roles in both academics and the workplace in a setting that is not contaminated by stereotyped notions.

FUTURE CHOICES: COLLEGE MAJOR, FUTURE PROFESSION

Do young women who attend single-sex middle or high schools show interest in different types of careers than those who attend co-educational schools? Some work suggests that they do. Solnick (1995) investigated the college major preference changes that occurred for young women who attended single-sex and co-educational colleges. In their first year of study, students indicated their intended college major. The researchers then followed up on the students to find out their actual major 4 years later. Her study showed that young women attending single-sex colleges who indicated they intended to major in traditionally female dominated subjects were more likely to switch out of such fields of study to more "neutral" or "male-dominated" fields than were their counterparts in co-educational colleges.

Lee and Marks (1990) also examined the college major choices, attitudes, values and behaviors of students who attended Catholic single-sex high schools or Catholic co-educational high schools. Analyses of their data showed that young women who had attended single-sex high schools tended to go to more selective colleges than their counterparts who had attended mixed-sex high schools and were more likely to be involved in an active way with politics by the end of college than their counterparts who had attended co-educational high schools (see Fig. 7.2).

Lee and Marks (1990) also analyzed students' plans for post-college education. Results showed that young women who had attended single-sex high schools were significantly more likely to consider going to law school (13.0%) than their counterparts who had attended co-educational high schools (7.7%). In contrast, young women who had attended mixed-sex high schools were significantly more likely to have never considered applying to graduate school (41.0%) than their counterparts who had attended single-sex high schools (31.3%). Analyses also indicated that young women who had attended single-sex high schools appeared to be more professionally ambitious than the young women who had attended co-educational secondary schools.

Results from a British sample showed similar patterns of career choices as a function of type of school. Lawrie and Brown (1992) showed that young women attending single-sex schools were more than twice as likely to predict that they would like to be a doctor (13%) than same-aged peers attending co-educational schools (5%; see Fig. 7.3). In contrast, young women attending co-educational schools indicated that they would be more likely to choose being a nurse (23%) than those in the single-sex school (13%). Lawrie and Brown (1992) found that type of school did not consistently affect the career preferences of the boys in their sample.

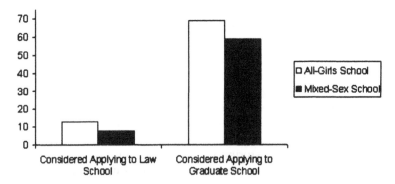

FIG. 7.2. Percent of young women who considered applying to law school and graduate school depending on type of high school attended (adapted from Lee & Marks, 1990). Copyright © 1990 by the American Psychological Association. Adapted with permission.

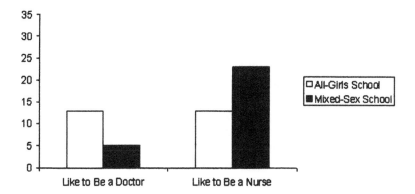

FIG. 7.3.   Percent of young women who would like to be a doctor versus a nurse in the future depending on type of high school attended (adapted from Lawrie & Brown, 1992).

In another study on the relationship between type of school and future outcomes, Riordan (1990) reported that young women graduating from single-sex colleges held more prestigious jobs than counterparts who had attended co-educational institutions.

Overall, the research presents some consistent patterns and some inconsistent ones. Results investigating the influence of single-sex schooling on young women's attitudes toward traditionally male-dominated topics consistently show benefits from single-sex settings. Young women in single-sex environments have more positive attitudes toward math and the physical sciences and also report more confidence in these areas than their same-sex counterparts attending mixed-sex schools. Results from actual academic performance per se paint a less consistent picture. It appears that under some conditions young women in single-sex schools outperform their peers in co-educational settings, but in other situations they do not. Importantly, single-sex schools appear to be correlated with less gender stereotypic plans for the future. And we have found no study in the literature that shows inferior academic performance by girls following single-sex education.

AN ALTERNATIVE APPROACH: THE SINGLE-SEX CLASSROOM

In general, we think that overall the research suggests that girls may benefit from single-sex academic environments, at least to some degree. Although we think that single-sex environments may have features that work for girls, there may also be important drawbacks to exclusively single-sex school settings. For instance, it is clearly important to prepare young people for the mixed-sex workplace, and more research should look at whether students who attend single-sex schools have difficulty adapting to mixed-sex settings in the future. Is there a way to preserve both the academic advantages of single-sex schools and the possible social advantages of co-educational schools? Recently, some educators have looked into the possibility that specialized single-sex classrooms within co-educational environments may be a way to derive the benefits seen in single-sex school environments while preserving the potential social advantages of co-educational environments. Single-sex classes have the advantage of letting young women learn about traditionally male-dominated areas of study in an environment where they may feel less competition for resources with boys, where they can secure attention from the teacher in equal amounts, and where they themselves may be less sex-typed. The idea of same-sex classes in areas other than physical education is recent, and there has been some research pointing to potential benefits from it. In the following subsection, we examine the studies that have looked at this topic.

Single-Sex Classrooms: Research

Choate Rosemary Hall is a highly regarded private secondary school in Wallingford, Connecticut. Teachers at the school decided to try an experiment with single-sex classrooms in science (Stowe, 1991). There were two Introduction to Physics classes taught at their school, one that was designed for the ninth/tenth grades and another designed for the eleventh/twelfth grades. During one academic year, the teachers made all of the physics classes same-sex. The comparison group in their study was comprised of students who had taken the identical physics courses the previous year in a mixed-sex environment. Students in the same-sex classes were not given advanced notice nor any explanation for the curriculum change, and the instructors attempted to teach the all-girls and all-boys classes similarly. At the end of the course, students were given follow-up questionnaires that were disguised as a standard, end-of-semester course evaluation form, and were asked to evaluate their experience. Responses from the students taking the same-sex physics classes were compared to those of students who had taken the identical course the previous year in a mixed-sex setting.

Stowe (1991) found some interesting results. Most striking was the number of girls who showed interest in pursuing physics-related careers. In surveys given before the physics classes, girls showed approximately the same interest in pursuing physics-related careers in the future regardless of whether they were taking the class in the experimental (same-sex) year or the control (mixed-sex) year. However, at the end of the semester after the course was completed, girls who had learned physics in all-female classes indicated significantly more interest in pursuing a physics-related career than girls who had learned the topic in mixed-sex classes the year before. Young women in the all-female classes also rated themselves as having participated more and as having enjoyed physics more than their counterparts in the mixed-sex classes of the previous year, although the differences between the single-sex and mixed-sex classes were not statistically significant for those two questions.

In addition, both boys and girls who had learned physics in the single-sex environment felt that their oral participation in the class was enhanced in the single-sex setting. Overall, this study suggests that single-sex classrooms have the potential to be a great success. The one drawback reported by Stowe (1991) was that both the young men and the young women reported less *enjoyment* of the single-sex class setting and thus did not recommend that the school continue it the following year.

A related study on single-sex mathematics classes showed gender differences in preference for single-sex learning environments. Jackson and Smith (2000) assessed girls' and boys' attitudes toward mathematics following single-sex mathematics instruction over a period of five school terms. The students had been given mathematics instruction in mixed-sex classes before the single-sex instruction began. Single-sex mathematics instruction began when the students were between the ages of 11 and 12 years, and ended when they were 12–13 years of age. Responses to questionnaire items following the instruction showed that girls overwhelmingly preferred their single-sex math classes—80% reported that they were more confident in single-sex classes, 65% reported that the single-sex environment fostered their progress in learning the material, and over 50% reported enjoying math more when in single-sex environments, whereas only 15% reported enjoying the mixed-sex settings more than the single-sex ones (see Fig. 7.4). In fact, Jackson and Smith (2000) reported that 80% of the girls preferred to continue with single-sex math instruction the following year.

Jackson and Smith (2000) also surveyed boys after the five-term single-sex instruction and found very interesting results. In contrast to the girls' overwhelming preference for single-sex classes, the boys in their study indicated a strong preference for mixed-sex mathematics environments. A large majority (64%) indicated that they did not want to continue the single-sex instruction the following year, and 72% expressed that they enjoyed mixed-sex settings to the single-sex ones. Although less dramatic, 33% of the boys expressed less confidence in boys-only groups.

Jackson and Smith's (2000) study raises some interesting questions about possible gender differences in preference for single- versus mixed-

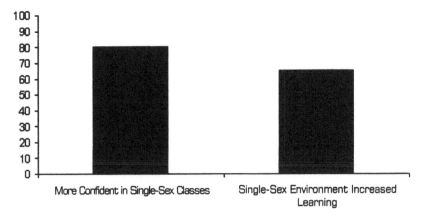

FIG. 7.4.   Percentage of girls in single-sex math classes reporting that they felt more confident and learned more in single-sex relative to mixed-sex (adapted from Jackson & Smith, 2000).

sex mathematics classroom environments. They conducted follow-up interviews with some of the students in an attempt to learn more about the students' reasons for preferring one type of classroom environment over another. Girls tended to report that they preferred single-sex classes because they felt more comfortable speaking up in class and were less concerned about the embarrassment that comes with expressing an incorrect answer aloud. One young woman in their study remarked, "I think I work better in single-sex, not with boys, because like you're embarrassed like if you get it wrong because they'll laugh …" (Jackson & Smith, 2000, p. 417). Boys, on the other hand, seemed to prefer mixed-sex classes because they felt that the girls had a calming effect on the classroom. One boy reported that the presence of girls in mixed-sex environments led him to get better grades because he ended up chatting with his friends less.

COMING TO RESOLUTION

We began our analysis of boys, girls, and the computer by focusing on two hypothetical children as they prepare to begin their long journey through the educational system. Our abiding concern has been whether the playing fields will be equal for Jared and Martha during that journey. They will each benefit from good and caring teachers, supportive parents, and well-financed schools. But with the increasing emphasis on technology and science in modern society, we see more dangers ahead for Martha than for Jared. In order for Martha to have the full range of choices available to her, she must overcome the barriers to success at technology. She must overcome the likelihood that she will soon have negative attitudes toward technology, an abundance of computer anxiety, and a self-image that tells her that she will never be as good at activities involving technology as she needs to be in order to compete with the boys. The road is not closed to her; it is just more difficult. Unless changes are made to our educational system, our advising, and our parenting, the likelihood is that Martha will succumb to the difficulty, becoming one more statistic in the digital divide.

Throughout the book, we have focused on a selected set of issues that affect girls in their pursuit of knowledge and comfort with technology. Girls must cope with inappropriate software in social contexts that exacerbate their anxiety. They must endure the expectations held by others that they are neither as competent nor as interested in technology as boys. Girls are taught to attribute any success at IT as being "just lucky," while they learn to attribute failure to lack of ability. As more girls opt out of technology courses and camps, the few who remain suffer from the effects of tokenism. In the end, the social stereotype establishes a burden that very few girls can successfully combat.

In chapter 6, we suggested some of the changes that can be made to enable teachers, parents, and school systems to become more aware of their contributions to the digital divide and empower them to even the playing field. In the current chapter, we thought it important to examine the most radical change—separating boys and girls by gender. There are clearly potential drawbacks to any suggestions for radical change in our educational system. Critics of single-sex education point to any number of potential adverse consequences. Indeed, those consequences may be real. However, the failure to take some action will necessarily continue the status quo. The girls who are growing up today cannot afford to be second-class citizens when it comes to technology. Society cannot afford the loss of social capital by disadvantaging half of its talent pool.

As research scientists, our mantra is that more research is needed. That is not a call for inaction. To the contrary, we believe that school systems should act on as many of the suggestions that we have made as possible, and others that we have not been sufficiently creative to generate. These include changes in teacher training to make the current educational system work better for girls and young women. However, public school districts and private schools should systematically create experiments in education through which they can test the efficacy of some of the more radical changes. We think that systems should experiment with at least voluntary single-sex schools and voluntary single-sex classrooms for technology, math, and science within co-educational settings. As Steele and his colleagues have shown us with the program at the University of Michigan (Steele, 1997), these opportunities must be presented as challenges rather than remediation. They must capture the imagination of people who want to break through the unwritten barriers rather than appear as segregated facilities for students who just cannot make it in traditional classrooms (see Willis & Kenway, 1986, for a thoughtful critique).

The digital divide by gender is harmful to females and harmful to society. There is cause for optimism if we seize the opportunity. We think that the time to act is now.

References

American Association of University Women. (1998a). *Gender gaps: Where schools still fail our children*. New York: Marlowe & Co.

American Association of University Women. (1998b). *Separated by sex: A critical look at single-sex education for girls*. Washington, DC: The Foundation.

American Association of University Women Educational Foundation Commission on Technology, Gender and Teacher Education. (2000). *Tech-Savvy: Educating girls in the new computer age*. Washington, DC: American Association of University Women Educational Foundation.

Anderson, F. S. (1999). The prediction and correlates of adolescent relationship identity. *Dissertation Abstracts International—B60(5-B)*: 2382.

Aronson, E. (1992). *Readings about the social animal*. New York : W. H. Freeman and Co.

Aronson, E., Stephan, C., Sikes, J., Blaney, N., & Snapp, M. (1978). *The Jigsaw Classroom*. Beverly Hills: Sage.

Aronson, J., Lustina, M. J., Good, C., Keough, K., Steele, C. M., & Brown, J. (1999). When White men can't do math: Necessary and sufficient factors in stereotype threat. *Journal of Experimental Social Psychology, 35*, 29–46.

Atwell, P., & Battle, J. (1999). Home computers and school performance. *The Information Society, 15*, 1–10.

Bank, B. J. (1995). Gendered accounts: Undergraduates explain why they seek their bachelor's degree. *Sex Roles, 32*, 527– 544.

Barbierri, M. S., & Light, P. (1992). Interaction, gender and performance on a computer-based problem solving task. *Learning and Instruction, 2*, 199–213.

Baroudi, J. J., & Igbaria, M. (1995). An examination of gender effects on career success of information systems employees. *Journal of Management Information Systems, 11*, 181–201.

Belle, D. (1989). *Children's social networks and social supports*. Oxford, England: John Wiley and Sons.

Brosnan, M. J. (1998). The impact of psychological gender, gender-related perceptions, significant others, and the introducer of technology upon computer anxiety in students. *Journal of Educational Computing Research, 18,* 63–78.

Brunner, C. (1997). Opening technology to girls. *Electronic Learning, 16,* 55.

Brutsaert, H., & Bracke, P. (1994). Gender context of the elementary school: Sex differences in affective outcomes. *Educational Studies, 20,* 3–11.

Burger, C. J., & Sandy, M. L. (1998). *A guide to gender fair education in science and mathematics.* Washington, DC: Office of Educational Research and Improvement.

Cairns, E. (1990). Impact of television news exposure on children's perceptions of violence in Northern Ireland. *Journal of Social Psychology, 130,* 447–452.

Campbell, P. B., & Storo, J. N. (1994). *Why me? Why my classroom?* Washington, DC: Office of Educational Research and Improvement.

Carpenter, P. W., & Hayden, M. (1987). Girls' academic achievements: Single-sex versus coeducational schools in Australia. *Sociology of Education, 60,* 156–167.

Chappel, K. K. (1996). Mathematics computer software characteristics with possible gender-specific impact: A content analysis. *Journal of Educational Computer Research, 15,* 25–35.

Chua, S. L., Chen, D. T., & Wong, A. F. L. (1999). Computer anxiety and its correlates: A meta-analysis. *Computers in Human Behavior, 15,* 609–623.

Clarke, V. A., & Chambers, S. M. (1989). Gender-based factors in computing enrollments and achievement: Evidence from a study of tertiary students. *Journal of Educational Computing Research, 5,* 409–429.

Cleary, C. (2002, February 10). Where the girls rule. *The Seattle Times,* p. A1.

Cohen, G. L., Steele, C. M., & Ross, L. D. (1999). The mentor's dilemma: Providing critical feedback across the racial divide. *Personality and Social Psychology Bulletin, 25,* 1302–1318.

College Board Statistics. (2001). *College Board, 2001.*

Colley, A. N., Gale, M. T., & Harris, T. A. (1994). Effects of gender role identity and experience on computer attitude components. *Journal of Educational Computing Research, 10,* 129–137.

Collis, B. A. (1987). Sex differences in the association between secondary school students' attitudes toward mathematics and toward computers. *Journal for Research in Mathematics Education, 18,* 394–402.

Coomber, C., Colley, A., Hargreaves, D. J., & Dorn, L. (1997). The effects of age, gender and computer experience upon computer attitudes. *Educational Research, 39,* 123–133.

Cooper, J. (1991). *Video arcades.* Unpublished manuscript, Princeton University.

Cooper, J., & Mackie, D. (1986). Video games and aggression in children. *Journal of Applied Social Psychology, 16,* 726–744.

Cooper, J., & Stone, J. (1996). Gender, computer-assisted learning, and anxiety: With a little help from a friend. *Journal of Educational Computing Research, 15,* 67–91.

Cooper, J., Hall, J., & Huff, C. (1990). Situational stress as a consequence of sex-stereotyped software. *Personality and Social Psychology Bulletin, 16,* 419–429.

Dalton, D., Hannafin, M. J., & Hooper, S. (1989). The effects of cooperative versus individualized instructional strategies on learning from computer-based instruction. *Educational Technology Research and Development, 37,* 15–24.

Dambrot, F. H., Watkins-Malek, M. A., Silling, S. M., Marshall, R. S., & Garver, J. A. (1985). Correlates of sex differences in attitudes toward and involvement with computers. *Journal of Vocational Behavior, 27,* 71–86.

Darley, J. M., & Latané, B. (1968). Bystander intervention emergencies: Diffusion of responsibility. *Journal of Personality and Social Psychology, 8,* 377–383.

Deaux, K. (1976). Sex: A perspective on the attribution process. In J. H. Harney, W. J. Ickes, & R. F. Kidd (Eds.), *New directions in attribution research* (Vol. 1, pp. 335–352). Hillsdale, NJ: Lawrence Erlbaum Associates.

Diener, C. I., & Dweck, C. S. (1978). An analysis of learned helplessness: Continuous changes in performance, strategy, and achievement cognitions following failure. *Journal of Personality and Social Psychology, 36,* 451–462.

Dweck, C. S. (1986). Motivational processes affecting learning. *American Psychologist, 41,* 1040–1048.

Dweck, C. S., Chiu, C., & Hong, Y. (1995). Implicit theories and their role in judgments and reactions: A world from two perspectives. *Psychological Inquiry, 6,* 267–285.

Dweck, C. S., & Reppucci, N. D. (1973). Learned helplessness and reinforcement responsibility in children. *Journal of Personality and Social Psychology, 25,* 109–116.

Eagly, A. H., & Kite, M. E. (1987). Are stereotypes of nationalities applied to both women and men? *Journal of Personality and Social Psychology, 53,* 451–462.

Farina, F., Arce, R., Sobral, J., & Carames, R. (1991). Predictors of anxiety towards computers. *Computers in Human Behavior, 7,* 263–267.

Frey, K. S., & Ruble, D. N. (1992). Gender constancy and the "cost" of sex-typed behavior: A test of the conflict hypothesis. *Developmental Psychology, 28,* 714–721.

Frieze, I. H. (1976). Causal attributions and information seeking to explain success and failure. *Journal of Research in Personality, 10,* 293–305.

Furger, R. (1998). *Does Jane compute?* New York: Warner Books.

Geis, F. L., Boston, M. B., & Hoffman, N. (1985). Sex of authority role models and achievement by men and women: Leadership performance and recognition. *Journal of Personality and Social Psychology, 49,* 636–653.

Granleese, J., & Joseph, J. (1993). Self-perception profile of adolescent girls at a single-sex and a mixed-sex school. *Journal of Genetic Psychology, 154,* 525–530.

Grayson, D., & Martin, M. (1988). *Gender expectations and student achievement: Teacher handbook.* Earlham, IA: GrayMill Foundation.

Gressard, C. P., & Loyd, B. H. (1986). The nature and correlates of computer anxiety in college students. *Journal of Human Behavior and Learning, 3,* 28–33.

Gwizdala, J., & Steinback, M. (1990). High school females' mathematics attitudes: An interim report. *School Science and Mathematics, 90,* 215–223.

Haberman, C. (2001, June 27). Tears of joy at a graduation for girls only. *New York Times,* p. B1.

Harvey, T. J., & Stables, A. (1986). Gender differences in attitudes to science for third-year pupils: An argument for single-sex teaching groups in mixed schools. *Research in Science and Technological Education, 4,* 163–170.

Hemenway, K. (1995). Human nature and the glass ceiling in industry. *Communications of the ACM, 38,* 1.

Higher Education Research Institute. (1996). *Graduate School of Education and Information Studies, The American Freshman: National Norms for Fall 1996.* Report, University of California, Los Angeles.

Huff, C., & Cooper, J. (1987). Sex bias in educational software: The effect of designers' stereotypes on the software they design. *Journal of Applied Social Psychology, 17,* 519–532.

Jacklin, C. N., & Maccoby, E. E. (1978). Social behavior at thirty-three months in same-sex and mixed-sex dyads. *Child Development, 49,* 557–569.

Jackson, C., & Smith, I. D. (2000). Poles apart? An exploration of single-sex and mixed-sex educational environments in Australia and England. *Educational Studies, 26,* 409–422.

Johnson, D. W., & Johnson, R. T. (1989). *Cooperation and competition: Theory and research.* Edina, MN: Interaction Book Co.

Johnson, D. W., Johnson, R. T., Richards, D. S., & Buckman, L. A. (1986). The effect of prolonged implementation of cooperative learning on social support within the classroom. *Journal of Psychology, 119,* 405–411.

Johnson, D. W., Maruyama, G., Johnson, R. T., Nelson, D., & Skon, L. (1981). Effects of cooperative, competitive, and individualistic goal structures on achievement: A meta analysis. *Psychological Bulletin, 89,* 47–62.

Johnson, R. T., Johnson, D. W., & Stanne, M. B. (1985). Effects of cooperative, competitive, and individualistic goal structures on computer-assisted instruction. *Journal of Educational Psychology, 77,* 668–677.

Jones, T., & Clarke, V. (1995). Diversity as a determinant of attitudes: A possible explanation of the apparent advantage of single-sex settings. *Journal of Educational Computing Research, 12,* 51–64.

Kaminer, W. (1998). The trouble with single sex schools. *Atlantic Monthly, April.*

Klawe, M., & Leveson, N. (1995). Women in computing: Where are we now? *Communications of the ACM, 38,* 1.

Kohlberg, L. (1966). A cognitive-developmental analysis of children's sex-role concepts and attitudes. In E. E. Maccoby (Ed.), *The development of sex differences* (pp. 82–173). Stanford, CA: Stanford University Press.

Latimer, C. P. (2001). *The digital divide: Understanding and addressing the challenge.* New York, NY: New York State Forum for Information Resource Management.

Lawrie, L., & Brown, R. (1992). Sex stereotypes, school subject preferences and career aspirations as a function of single/mixed-sex schooling and presence/absence of an opposite sex sibling. *British Journal of Educational Psychology, 62,* 132–138.

Lee, V. E., & Bryk, A. S. (1986). Effects of single-sex secondary schools on student achievement and attitudes. *Journal of Educational Psychology, 78,* 381–395.

Lee, V. E., & Lockheed, M. E. (1990). The effects of single-sex schooling on achievement and attitudes in Nigeria. *Comparative Education Review, 34,* 209–231.

Lee, V. E., & Marks, H. M. (1990). Sustained effects of the single-sex secondary school experience on attitudes, behaviors, and values in college. *Journal of Educational Psychology, 82,* 578–592.

LePore, P. C., & Warren, J. R. (1997). A comparison of single-sex and coeducational Catholic secondary schooling: Evidence from the National Educational Longitudinal Study of 1988. *American Educational Research Journal, 34*, 485–511.

Lepper, M. R., & Malone, T. W. (1987). Intrinsic motivation and instructional effectiveness in computer-based education. In R. E. Snow & M. J. Farr (Eds.), *Aptitude, learning and instruction: Vol. 3. Conative and affective process analysis.* Hillsdale, NJ: Lawrence Erlbaum Associates.

Licht, B. G., & Dweck, C. S. (1984). Determinants of academic achievement: The interaction of children's achievement orientations with skill area. *Developmental Psychology, 20*, 628–636.

Light, P., Littleton, K., Bale, S., Joiner, R., & Messer, D. (2000). Gender and social comparison effects in computer-based problem solving. *Learning and Instruction, 10*, 483–496.

Lichtman, J. (1998). The Cyber Sisters Club: Using the Internet to bridge the technology gap with inner city girls. *T.H.E. Journal, 26*, 47.

Littleton, K., Light, P., Joiner, R., Messer, D., & Barnes, P. (1992). Pairing and gender effects on children's compute-based learning. *European Journal of Psychology of Education, 7*, 311–324.

Littleton, K., Light, P., Joiner, R., Messer, D., & Barnes, P. (1998). Gender, task scenarios and children's computer-based problem solving. *Educational Psychology, 18*, 327–340.

Lord, C., & Saenz, D. S. (1985). Memory deficits and memory surfeits. Differential cognitive consequences of tokenism for tokens and observers. *Journal of Personality and Social Psychology, 49*, 918–926.

Maccoby, E. E. (1990). Gender and relationships: A development account. *American Psychologist, 45*, 513–520.

Mael, F. A. (1998). Single-sex and coeducational schooling: Relationships to socioemotional and academic development. *Review of Educational Research, 68*, 101–129.

Marsh, H. W. (1991). Public, Catholic single-sex, and Catholic coeducational high Schools: Their effects on achievement, affect, and behaviors. *American Journal of Education, 99*, 320–356.

Marsh, H. W. (1989). Effects of attending single-sex and coeducational high schools on achievement, attitudes, behaviors and sex differences. *Educational Psychology, 81*, 70–85.

Martin, R. (1991). Schoolchildren's attitudes toward computers as a function of gender, course subjects and availability of home computers. *Journal of Computer-Assisted Learning, 7*, 187–194.

Matthews, J. (1988). *Escalante: The best teacher in America.* New York: Henry Holt & Co.

Mattson, P. O. (1960). Communicated anxiety in a two person situation. *Journal of Consulting Psychology, 24*, 488–495.

McClelland, M. (2001). Closing the IT gap for race and gender. *Journal of Educational Computing Research, 25*, 5–15.

McGuire, W. J., & McGuire, C. V. (1981). The spontaneous self-concept as affected by personal distinctiveness. In M. D. Lynch, A. Norem-Hebeisen, & K. J. Gergen

(Eds.), *Self-concept: Advances in theory and research* (pp. 147–171). Cambridge, MA: Ballinger.

Michaels, J. W., Blommel, J. M., Brocato, R. M., Linkous, R. A., & Rowe, J. S. (1982). Social facilitation and inhibition in a natural setting. *Replications in Social Psychology (now Contemporary Social Psychology), 2,* 21–24.

Miller, D. T., Taylor, B., & Buck, M. L. (1991). Gender gaps: Who needs to be explained? *Journal of Personality and Social Psychology, 61,* 5–12.

Miller-Bernal, L. (1993). Single-sex versus coeducational environments: A comparison of women students' experiences at four colleges. *American Journal of Education, 102,* 23–54.

National Coalition of Girls' Schools (2000). Fall Data Survey. Retrieved February 28, 2003, from http://www.ncgs.org

Nelson, L. J., & Cooper, J. (1997). Gender differences in children's reactions to success and failure with computers. *Computers in Human Behavior, 13,* 247–267.

Nelson, L. J., Weise, G. M., & Cooper, J. (1991). Getting stared with computers: Experience, anxiety, and relational style. *Computers in Human Behavior, 7,* 185–202.

Newman, L. S., Ruble, D. N., & Cooper, J. (1995). Gender and computers: II. The interactive effects of knowledge and constancy on gender-stereotyped attitudes. *Sex Roles, 33,* 325–351.

Nicholls, J. G. (1975). Causal attributions and other achievement-related cognitions: Effects of task outcome, attainment value, and sex. *Journal of Personality and Social Psychology, 31,* 379–389.

Okebukola, P. A., & Woda, A. B. (1993). The gender factor in computer anxiety and interest among some Australian high school students. *Educational Research, 35,* 181–189.

Panteli, N., Stack, J., & Ramsay, H. (2001). Gendered patterns in computing work in the late 1990s. *New Technology, Work and Employment, 16,* 3–17.

Papadakis, E. (2000). Environmental values and political action. *Journal of Sociology, 36,* 81–97.

Parsons, J. E., Meece, J. L., Adler, T. F., & Kaczala, C. M. (1982). Sex differences in attributions and learned helplessness. *Sex Roles, 8,* 421–432.

Plaut, V. C., Cheryan, S., Rios, K. M., & Steele, C. M. (2003, February). *Diversifying sociocultural representations of computer science to increase women's participation.* Poster session presented at the annual meeting of the Society for Personality and Social Psychology, Los Angeles, CA.

Polimeni, A. M., Hardie, E., & Buzwell, S. (2002). Friendship closeness inventory: Development and psychometric evaluation. *Psychological Reports, 91,* 142–152.

Powlishta, K. K. (1987, April). *The social context of cross-sex interactions.* Paper presented at biennial meeting of the Society for Research in Child Development, Baltimore, MD.

Reinen, I. J., & Plomp, T. (1997). Information technology and gender equality: A contradiction in terminis? *Computers and Education, 28,* 65–78.

Riordan, C. H. (1990). *Girls and boys in school: Together or separate?* New York: Teachers College Press.

Robinson-Staveley, K., & Cooper, J. (1990). Mere presence, gender, and reactions to computers: Studying human-computer interaction in the social context. *Journal of Experimental Social Psychology, 26,* 168–183.

Rosenthal, R., & Jacobson, L. (1968). Pygmalion in the classroom: Teacher expectation and pupil's intellectual development. New York: Holt, Rinehart & Winston.

Rudman, L. A., & Glick, P. (1999). Prescriptive gender stereotypes and backlash toward agentic women. *Journal of Social Issues, 57,* 743–762.

Sadker, M., & Sadker, D. (1994*). Failing at fairness: How America's schools cheat girls.* New York: C. Scribner's Sons.

Schmader, T. (2002). Gender identification moderates stereotype threat effects on women's math performance. *Journal of Experimental Social Psychology, 38,* 194–201.

Schlechter, T. (1990). The relative instructional efficiency of small group computer-based telecommunications for instruction. *Journal of Computer-Based Instruction, 6,* 329–341.

Schofield, J. W. (1995). *Computers and classroom culture.* Cambridge: Cambridge University Press.

Selwyn, N. (1998). The effect of using a home computer on students' educational use of it. *Computers and Education, 31,* 211–227.

Serbin, L. A., Sprafkin, C., Elman, M., & Doyle, A. B. (1982). The early development of sex-differentiated patterns of social influence. *Canadian Journal of Behavioural Science, 14,* 350–363.

Shih, M., Pittinsky, T. L., & Ambady, N. (1999). Stereotype susceptibility: Identity salience and shifts in quantitative performance. *Psychological Science, 10,* 80–83.

Signorella, M. L., Frieze, I. H., & Hershey, S. W. (1996). Single-sex versus mixed-sex classes and gender schemata in children and adolescents. *Psychology of Women Quarterly, 20,* 599–607.

Slaby, R. G., & Frey, K. S. (1975). Development of gender constancy and selective attention to same-sex models. *Child Development, 46,* 849–856.

Smith, D. G. (1990). Women's colleges and coed colleges: Is there a difference for Women? *Journal of Higher Education, 61,* 181–197.

Snyder, M., Tanke, E., & Berscheid, E. (1977). Social perception and interpersonal behavior: On the self-fulfilling nature of social stereotypes. *Journal of Personality and Social Psychology, 35,* 656–666.

Solnick, S. (1995). Changes in women's majors from entrance to graduation at women's and coeducational colleges. *Industrial and Labor Relations Review, 48,* 505–514.

Spencer, S. J., Steele, C. M., & Quinn, D. M. (1999). Stereotype threat and women's math performance. *Journal of Experimental Social Psychology, 35,* 4–28.

Stables, A. (1990). Differences between pupils from mixed and single-sex schools in their enjoyment of school subjects in their attitudes to science and to school. *Educational Review, 42,* 221–230.

Steele, C. M. (1997). A threat in the air: How stereotypes shape intellectual identity and performance. *American Psychologist, 52,* 613–629.

Steele, C. M., & Aronson, J. (1995). Stereotype threat and the intellectual test performance of African Americans. *Journal of Personality and Social Psychology, 69,* 797–811.

Stephenson, S. D. (1994). The use of small groups in computer-based training: A review of recent literature. *Computers in Human Behavior, 10,* 243–259.

Stone, J., Lynch, C. I., Sjomeling, M., & Darley, J. M. (1999). Stereotype threat effects on Black and White athletic performance. *Journal of Personality and Social Psychology, 77,* 1213–1227.

Stone, J., Perry, Z. W., & Darley, J. M. (1997). "White men can't jump": Evidence for the perceptual confirmation of racial stereotypes following a basketball game. *Basic and Applied Social Psychology, 19,* 291–306.

Stowe, L. G. (1991). Should physics classes be single sex? *Physics Teacher, 29,* 380–381.

Stricker, L., & Rock, D. A. (1995). Examinee background characteristics and GRE general test performance. *Intelligence, 21,* 49–67.

Temple, L., & Lips, H. M. (1989). Gender differences and similarities in attitudes toward computers. *Computers in Human Behavior, 5,* 215–226.

Thompson, S. K. (1975). Gender labels and early sex role development. *Child Development, 46,* 339–347.

Tiedemann, J. (2000). Parents' gender stereotypes and teachers' beliefs as predictors of children's concept of their mathematical ability in elementary school. *Journal of Educational Psychology, 92,* 144–151.

Tijdens, K. G. (1997). Behind the screens: The foreseen and unforeseen impact of computerization on female office worker's jobs. *Gender, Work, and Organization, 6,* 47–57.

Todman, J., & Dick, G. (1993). Primary children and teacher's attitudes to computers. *Computers and Education, 20,* 199–203.

"Trying to predict the future." *Popular Computing, 3,* 30–44.

Turkle, S., & Papert, S. (1990). Epistemological pluralism: Styles and voices within the computer culture. *Signs, 16,* 128–157.

U.S. Department of Education (1992). Cooperative learning. *Office of Research Education Consumer Guide.* Washington, DC: Author.

U.S. Department of Education (1996). *Digest of Education Statistics, 1996.* Washington, DC: Author.

U.S. Department of Education (2000). *1999–2000 National Postsecondary Student Aid Study.* Washington, DC: Author.

U.S. Department of Education (2002, May 1). Press release: Secretary Paige announces intent to provide more flexibility regarding single-sex classes and schools.

Virginia Space Grant Consortium (1996). *Gender equity awareness training module with classroom strategies for mathematics, science and technology.* Hampton, VA: Author.

Weil, M. M., Rosen, L. D., & Sears, D. C. (1987). The computerphobia reduction program: Year 1. Program development and preliminary results. *Behavior Research Methods, Instruments and Computers, 19,* 180–184.

Weiner, B. (1979). A theory of motivation for some classroom experiences. *Journal of Educational Psychology, 71,* 3–25.

Weiner, B. (1986). *An attributional theory of motivation and emotion*. New York: Springer-Verlag.

Weiner, B., Frieze, I., Kukla, A., Reed, L., Rest, B., & Rosenbaum, R. M. (1971). *Perceiving the causes of success and failure*. Morristown, NJ: General Learning Press.

Whitley, B. E., Jr. (1997). Gender differences in computer-related attitudes and behavior: A meta-analysis. *Computers in Human Behavior, 13*, 1–22.

Wilder, G., Mackie, D., & Cooper, J. (1985). Gender and computers: Two surveys of computer-related attitudes. *Sex Roles, 13*, 215–228.

Willis, S., & Kenway, J. (1986). On overcoming sexism in schooling: To marginalize or mainstream. *Australian Journal of Education, 30*, 132–149.

Word, C. O., Zanna, M. P., & Cooper, J. (1974). The nonverbal mediating of self-fulfilling prophecies in interracial interaction. *Journal of Experimental Social Psychology, 10*, 109–120.

Wright, R., & Jacobs, J. A. (1994). Male flight from computer work: A new look at re-segregation and ghettoization. In J. A. Jacobs (Ed.), *Gender inequality at work* (pp. 334–378). London: Sage.

Young, D. J., & Fraser, B. J. (1990). Science achievement of girls in single-sex and co-educational schools. *Research in Science and Technological Education, 8*, 5–20.

Author Index

Subject Index